Madam Warden

This book is dedicated to:

Perry Johnson, who decided to introduce women into Michigan Corrections in a thoughtful and planned way, and who supported their journeys and monitored their progress to guide them to success,

and Bill Kime, the love of my life, without whom there would have been no book,

and John Cordell, who inspired me to get my act together and has been a joy in my life,

and Luella Burke, Tekla Miller, and Denise Quarles, without whose support I would not have survived Jackson to become a warden.

Madam Warden
Pamela K. Withrow
A Memoir of the First Woman in
 Michigan to Head a Prison for Men

Author: Pamela K. Withrow
Editor: Tanya Muzumdar
Designer: Kelly Ludwig
Cover design: Sarah Meiers

Readers are encouraged to go to www. MissionPointPress.com to contact the author or to find information on how to buy this book in bulk at a discounted rate.

MISSION POINT PRESS

Published by Mission Point Press
2554 Chandler Rd.
Traverse City, MI 49696
(231) 421-9513
www.MissionPointPress.com

ISBN: 978-1-958363-39-3

Library of Congress Control Number:
2022917224

Printed in the United States of America

Madam Warden

A Memoir of the First
Woman in Michigan
to Head a Prison for Men

Pamela K. Withrow

Madam Warden is a richly detailed memoir of Pam's life and exemplary career. She acquaints the reader with all aspects of personal and professional skills, competencies, and the courage required to achieve organizational change regardless of the age, size, security level, and history of a prison.

—*Sharon Johnson Rion, retired CEO of TransCor*
and former warden in the US and England

Pam Withrow has left an invaluable account of a career in the very male Department of Corrections at the crucial point when women began to take positions of leadership, giving the reader a lively account of three sources of support—innovative male mentors, supportive women colleagues, and professional organizations—that worked to counter the antipathy that greeted this woman pioneer. The reader comes to understand how Withrow was able to promote humane facilities for prisoners and staff by dint of her own quiet methods, strategizing, and tireless work.

—*Leslie Page Moch, professor of history emerita, Michigan State University*

CONTENTS

Foreword 01

Preface..03

1.   The Making of This Warden..05

2.   Prisons I Have Known...16

3.   Offender Programs: Changing Hearts and Minds 21

4.   One Prisoner's Story of Change...31

5.   When Things Go Wrong..43

6.   When Things Go Right...48

7.   Prisoners Who Made an Impression 54

8.   Prison Coworkers: Outstanding and Not So Wonderful.........64

9.   Twenty-Five Years in Prison: Lessons Learned......................75

Acknowledgments 81

About the Author 83

FOREWORD

"When I grow up, I want to be a prison warden."

How many people have you heard state that as their career path? My guess is not many. Add to it that the professional is a female, and I'd wager that number drops even lower.

The material in this book not only delves deeply into the journey of becoming a warden, it tackles the very challenging and difficult path of being a woman in a traditionally male-dominated field. Within these pages, she discusses the concept of concrete correctional practices, as well as the journey of a woman learning how to maneuver herself in a foreign work environment, with the aim of providing teachable moments to educate us all on how to be successful at both.

As a university educator and former warden, I found this book important in conveying correctional concepts in an easily digestible manner. As a woman, I found it touching, humorous, painful, and exhilarating as I walked along with Pam through her life and career.

—Patty Barnhart, former prison warden, and lecturer, Arizona State University

PREFACE

As an Indiana farm girl, my aspiration was to be an English teacher. My family moved to Michigan when I was a senior in high school. A promising start at Michigan State University ended when I was raped at a party and made a half-hearted suicide attempt. Next thing I knew, I was a teen mother, half of a failing marriage, and desperate to return to college. Your tax dollars opened that door. Money from a federal program for improving law enforcement provided books and tuition at Lansing Community College and MSU; state welfare provided living expenses. An element of the law enforcement funding offered loan forgiveness if I worked in the field for four years.

It was a quirk of fate that led me to prison work. I was divorced and dating a bus driver who asked his passengers if anyone knew of a job for his girlfriend who had a criminal justice degree. A guy working for Corrections said, "I think we are starting to hire women." And that is how I found myself interviewing for a job in the prison business.

First stop was Personnel at the Corrections Department headquarters. The affirmative action officer said, "Why don't you go to the Camp Program and talk to Superintendent Butchko?" I did. The superintendent was not interested. Back to Personnel. The affirmative action officer said, "Aren't you on that program that will pay your salary for six months?"

I was. He made a call and the next interview with Superintendent Butchko ended with a job offer. I still remember Butchko telling me, while offering a counselor position, "I intended to get six months work out of you and let you go, but you earned this job." And that started a twenty-five-year career full of surprises.

This book was conceived by my husband, Bill Kime, who thought the story of the first woman to run a prison for men should be told. As a result, I kept boxes of files and calendars. When Bill passed, I started writing to honor his memory, but I kept writing because he was only partly right. It is true that I survived various trials to become Michigan's first female to supervise a prison housing men. The rest of the story is that I loved working in prisons; the staff and prisoners created endless puzzles to solve, and every prison had its own culture and personality. The challenge of taking often dysfunctional operations and creating facilities that worked well and met the needs of those working and living in them was a joy.

Because there are so many myths and stereotypes about prisons, I decided to tell my truth about prison work, why I stayed with it, and what I learned in twenty-five years in the business.

1. THE MAKING OF THIS WARDEN

Just as no mother looks at her baby and says, "I sure hope this child grows up to become a prisoner," few people focus their studies on correctional management. I have met many wardens and have yet to find one who intended, while a college student, to make prison management their life work. Most learn, as I did, through progressively responsible jobs. Let me describe my "training" to be a prison warden.

In 1976 the Camp Program headquarters was near Jackson, and my first office was shared with an inmate clerk. That clerk lived in one of the twelve small prisons overseen by a superintendent and his staff. Many of these mini-prisons were converted prisoner-of-war camps, hence the term "Camp" Program. The inmate was charged with teaching me his job, which was to order eyeglasses and orthopedic shoes for his fellow prisoners, so that I could take it over. He was a pleasant guy who seemed vaguely amused at this assignment. Noting that those tasks would not fill an eight-hour day, my boss said, "Read inmate files to get a sense of the type of prisoner housed in the Camp Program and the way files are organized."

So, I spent most of three months across the hall in the records office reading files. This make-work job had been offered, reluctantly, because my salary was paid by a federal program designed to get welfare mothers into the workforce. While Superintendent Frank Buchko did not want a woman in a counselor position, free help was not going to be refused. When a classified civil service job came open, I interviewed and was offered the position. All the file reading paid off because I now added processing corrections center, work pass, and furlough applications to my daily tasks. No one taught me how to handle these; I read policies and procedures to figure out how to do the work.

»»»»»»»»»»»»»

Next door to the headquarters building was Camp Waterloo. Workers from the camp were friendly and polite and I was curious about their living conditions. Their camp supervisor often visited my office, and I asked him about his operation. He was a bit of a renegade and one day said, "Want a tour of the camp?" I knew the unwritten rule that women did not go there but could not resist the chance. "Yes," I said, and off we went, right through a forbidden door and into his domain. Long dormitories, lined with bunks, comprised the living quarters. There was a dining hall, kitchen, offices, and a visiting area. I do not recall much more about that visit, except that I detected the faint odor of marijuana. "I smell dope," I said. His response was laconic. "It's not a big problem and it keeps the inmates quiet."

It was not all drudgery, though. There was fun to be had at the quarterly staff meetings. These were held at the McMullen Training Center near Higgins Lake State Park and brought the twelve camp supervisors together for two days—meetings during the day, and hard partying at night. Here my corrections education continued, since most of the supervisors had worked at one of Michigan's old penitentiaries (Jackson, Marquette, or the Reformatory) prior to their promotions to head camps. Of course, I had many questions about their prison experiences, but also learned to listen to the stories. For example, "Your reputation will be damaged forever if you offer rioting inmates steak and ice cream." Other tales were funny or sad recollections of staff or prisoners they had come to know over the years. The lesson here was that everybody in a prison is a person just trying to get through the day as best they can.

At one camp supervisors' meeting, John Hawley proclaimed, "Withrow, you're gonna make a hell of a corrections man someday." That felt like a blessing because John was known to be an excellent supervisor. The fact that I would never be a man was lost in the sentiment; however, gender was, and continued to be, an issue as I moved up in the department. One headquarters coworker even said, "I don't think women should work around male prisoners; their presence is disruptive to the good order needed to operate a prison." That seemed a little over the top in a minimum-security setting where inmates mopped floors and emptied the trash.

After about a year, I was asked to interview for a job in the Program Bureau at Corrections's headquarters. Unbeknownst to me, Superintendent Butchko had called Deputy Director Kime to recommend me, saying, "I know you are always looking for bright kids for your area. I've got one for you."

Kime later told me, "I knew Butchko was no fan of women and if he was recommending one, she had to be special." I was hired on the spot; however, Kime said things were a little slow. "Read files for a while to get a feel for the kinds of work the Program Bureau handles." That had a familiar ring. He offered two three-shelf lateral files, each about four feet long, and suggested I begin with anything that looked interesting. Well, everything looked interesting, so I started at the beginning and worked my way through all the files. It took about a month. When I was done, I reported to Kime, "I've read the files." His response was, "All of them?" Well, I had.

He then found a small project that involved some basic research and a simple report. I finished that and submitted it through my nominal boss, Kime's assistant. He returned it with only a few red-pen suggestions from Kime. The assistant asked, "How did this get through the boss with so few corrections?" Later, I found that he was not a strong writer and that his submissions usually were returned with lots of arrows, deletions, and rewording. That this new kid on the block had managed to generally satisfy his boss had to have been galling. Of course, since I had just spent a month reading files, I had a good idea of the kind of writing the Bureau produced and had tried to keep my report consistent with that standard. Kime was happy; his assistant was not. That was to be true during the whole of my tenure in Lansing. Other assignments came quickly.

One that prepared me for my next position was prompted by the director's need for an assessment of new corrections officer training. Since female officers were still relatively new to the department, he suggested that I might be the right person for that task. Off I went to Jackson. I was dreading the tour of the cell blocks. These were concrete and steel units, five tiers high, with barred cell fronts and over two hundred men on each side. The officers' station had a plexiglass overhang to prevent staff from being pelted with items thrown from the cells. Women were not allowed to work as officers in the blocks; as the only woman in the class, I feared catcalls or other abuse. It was frightening to walk the narrow catwalks outside the cells. You could feel the hostility of the inmates as we passed, as some prisoners positioned themselves against the bars, glaring at us with hands gripping the bars so tightly their knuckles were white. As it turned out, there was a slender young man in the class who wore his blond hair in a style well below his collar. The inmates singled him out, with calls of: "Blondie, Blondie, Blondie," and offers that were quite obscene in nature. He returned to class the next day with a buzz cut.

In 1977, corrections officers received two weeks of training in the classroom and then were sent to the prison where they would be assigned for on-the-job training, which included firearms qualifications. Lt. Ames was the range instructor. He asked, "You shoot much?" "Been deer hunting," was my response. He then treated me no differently than the other trainees and I qualified with the rifle, shotgun, and handgun. Next stop would be working as an officer, paired with an experienced female.

While the training director had been told about my assignment, none of the trainers knew I was evaluating their performance. There was work waiting for me at the Program Bureau and I was writing the assessment as the training progressed, so I did not plan to spend all the on-the-job training days at Jackson—my assigned prison. So, I went to work as an officer for a few days and then went to Lansing for a day. When I returned and reported in, Captain Roby said, "See me after roll call."

What the captain wanted to see me about was the previous day's absence. I had assumed that he knew of my assignment as a training evaluator. It turned out that he did not know, or care, about that. He told me, "If you need to miss work, you call the control center and tell the sergeant why you won't be coming in."

I stammered, "But, I am not a regular trainee; I'm auditing the training." I suspect he was angry that he had not been told of my role. This experience prepared me for many instances in the future when incomplete or inconsistent communications would cause problems. Whether written or verbal, clear, complete communication is essential to getting prison work done right. It became my mission to make sure staff with whom I worked got information from me that would make it easier, not harder, to get the job done.

»»»»»»»»»»»»

My stint at Jackson opened my eyes to officer involvement in prisoner misconduct. One of the approved assignments for a female officer was the visiting room. While assigned there, I observed an unusual prisoner act. "That guy and his visitor just exchanged shoes. Is that allowed?" I asked my mentor. She responded, "New shoes are hard to get in prison." Since I knew nothing about how prisoners got personal clothing, I accepted her response; however, I later asked one of the supervisors about the event.

He frowned. "No, that was a violation. The prisoner was probably getting drugs as well as new shoes in that transaction."

On another occasion, the same female officer permitted a prisoner and his female visitor to occupy the bathroom at the same time, although they did not enter together. Even though I was a "fish" (new officer or new prisoner), I knew this was not right. "Officer, a mistake has occurred. A prisoner and his visitor are in the bathroom together." She had to intervene, and I allowed her to save face by calling it a mistake. I had learned another prison survival skill: calling a violation a mistake when dealing with a peer permits you to identify a problem and let the other person fix it before you both get into trouble.

The last time I was with that same officer was in a hall. As she passed a prisoner, I heard her call out: "I will pick up that carton of squares at the end of the shift."

I may have been a fish, but I knew she was referring to a carton of cigarettes. I also knew that prisoners treated these as currency and that she was being paid off for permitting a rule violation. I reported all these events to supervisors but have no way of knowing whether any disciplinary action ensued. Years later, when discussing my observations with her coworkers and supervisors, I found that she was generally known to be colluding with prisoners to break the rules and was so good at it that she was never caught. I also know that this officer later earned a degree and became a supervisor, which is a sad testament to the practice of rewarding education and longevity with promotion, without regard to character issues.

While most learning took place during office hours, I also gained knowledge at the after-work gatherings. With alcohol as a lubricant, people would tell stories about the work of corrections—and sometimes the misdeeds of coworkers. It was at one of these parties that I heard about the warden who had smashed up his state car while driving under the influence. The car was taken to a prison with an auto-body repair vocational program, fixed, painted, and returned to the warden without any formal report to Central Office. I discovered that another warden, who was "promoted" to a desk in the hall in Central Office until he decided to retire, had received that "promotion" because of his ill-treatment of his assistant deputy, who leapfrogged over him to become the deputy director in charge of all the prisons. The lesson there was to be fair to everyone because you never knew who your boss would be. The other thing I learned at those parties, and in my day-to-day dealings, was that the people in Central Office are regular folks who struggle with problems and issues. They have experience and knowledge that suit them for their jobs, but they are not miracle workers and do not have all the answers. The last thing I learned was that I was not suited for Central Office. Long meetings that left issues unresolved were frustrating to me; I have one of those faces unsuitable for poker—what I am thinking is written all over it. When what you are thinking is something like, "Will this meeting never end?" or "Why can't someone just decide so we can move on?" you know you need to find a different job.

Fortunately, the next job was at Camp Brighton. Unfortunately, I was named the supervisor of the camp without any previous supervisory experience and only new officer training as custody background. I was sent to find the camp on my own and was met in the parking lot by a reporter from the *Brighton Argus*. Someone in Central Office had alerted *Argus* staff to this first woman appointment. I had no training for dealing with the media. I answered the reporter's questions briefly and honestly, and posed for a photo with a very pregnant beagle who had ambled out to meet us.

After going inside to meet the staff, I spotted the count board. I said, "Tell me how that works," revealing to the desk officer my ignorance about this basic tool, used throughout each day to ensure all prisoners are present and accounted for. The lieutenant cleared his throat. "Perhaps we should start with a tour." He introduced me to the day-shift staff and showed me the rest of the camp. When the afternoon sergeant arrived, he, the lieutenant, and I went into the inner office, which I later learned was called the "pine box."

I thought I had considered all the possible problems I'd encounter at the camp, but was astounded when the sergeant announced, using theatrical gestures to punctuate his speech: "I will give you my usual 110 percent until you hang yourself, and then I want to be the one to pull the trap door."

There were three of us standing in the small office. The sergeant was six feet, two inches, and I was five feet, four inches. Feeling somewhat intimidated, I responded, "I hope you'll give me a chance," and turned to the lieutenant for more transitional information. He did not fail me and continued his description of camp operations as if nothing had happened.

As I got to know them, I said to staff, "I know people in Lansing and at Camp Control who can make camp life better. I'll work those angles if you'll teach me to run a camp." So, we came to an accommodation. Things were going well for several months and then—disaster! The lieutenant, who was the only actively supportive staff member, separated a shoulder trying to break a horse and was unable to return to prison work. I was left with the sergeant as acting lieutenant. As quickly as possible, I hired a permanent replacement. While the sergeant had potential, there was no way I could make him lieutenant so soon after his confrontational greeting. Instead, I hired an experienced lieutenant who kept the camp running well while I learned the craft of being camp supervisor, which included being the counselor to 140 prisoners. The dual responsibilities of staff supervision and counseling offenders were challenging. I was glad I had been told to read inmate files and had gained experience with furlough, work pass, and correction center applications during my first assignment. At least I knew the rudiments of those processes. From policy and procedure manuals, I learned to write parole eligibility reports and how to prepare offenders to meet with the parole board.

Then it was time for the quarterly supervisors' meeting. The first one was interesting. Most of the supervisors were frosty. I knew John Andrews, since Camp Waterloo was next door to Camp Control. He and Duane Corey, from Camp Lehman, were two who made a point of offering to be resources. In addition, they provided evening companionship, where the entertainment continued to involve alcoholic beverages and snacks in a common area while swapping prison stories.

One of those evenings, Andrews and Corey decided we should take some beer and cruise the back roads looking for deer. It was Corey's territory, and deer season was approaching. They both lit cigars, and, as the pickup cab filled with smoke, I recall asking for a cigar. "Gimme one of those. If I have to smell it, I might as well taste it too." To my amazement, I liked the taste and became a periodic cigar smoker, even though I abhorred cigarettes and did not allow smoking in the pine box. The cigar smoking would become my trademark. Before smoking was banned departmentwide, I would knit and smoke at meetings.

»»»»»»»»»»»»

Then there were riots at Jackson, Marquette, and the Reformatory. I learned that there would be investigations following these disturbances and the warden and his staff would be removed if found to be responsible for the uprisings. To my dismay, I got a call. "Go to Jackson and interview for the warden's administrative assistant position."

By this time, I had figured out that Director Johnson was responsible for my selection as Camp Brighton's supervisor and was now moving me into a new role. I felt I had mastered the role of camp supervisor and understood minimum-security operations but knew little about a secure facility. As the warden's representative, I needed to appear competent and in control. This was difficult because I knew so little about how this penitentiary operated. It was true that I had attended new officers' school at Jackson, but I did not work as an officer inside the secure perimeter, so was unfamiliar with the physical layout.

As in the past, good staff came to my aid. Charley Anderson, who had once served as Jackson's warden, said, "People will try to make an issue of your gender; let that be their problem." As one of the early Black appointees in Corrections, he certainly had the perspective to offer that advice.

Later, when I became assistant deputy warden for housing in Central Complex, the man I was replacing patiently went through the responsibilities of the position. "Many of these tasks are not part of my job," he said. "They were piled on because administrators were trying to get rid of me. Ditch them as quickly as possible." That was a kind act on his part, and I was touched that he had the integrity to help me during a time of personal disgrace.

Later, I realized that his move to Trustee Division, the minimum-security part of Jackson, improved his quality of life immeasurably, and that I had inherited an awful job. Getting work done was hampered by the fact that there were no bathroom facilities for women inside the prison. The deputy had a private bathroom in his office, which he would let the women use except when his door was closed. That was a signal to stay out. Traversing the security gates to and from the public restroom took nearly half an hour. Given that Jackson ran on coffee, multiple daily trips were needed. The women in the office considered me a hero when I managed to get a mop closet converted to a restroom.

That issue aside, I was drowning! Nothing at Brighton had prepared me for the crushing workload at Jackson. I knew I needed to follow policy, but signing logbooks in seven cell blocks, making even a cursory inspection of each, and talking with staff was a full day! I would work late to catch up on office duties. Not surprisingly, my personal life was suffering badly. In despair, I met with Director Johnson. "I can't do the job; please let me return to Camp Brighton," I pleaded. He responded, "Don't worry about it, sis; nobody's ever been able to do that job. Just do your best."

I went back and gave it my best for a couple more weeks. No improvement. I tried again to convince the director that I was just not cut out for Jackson. In frustration, I even cried, something I had never done at work. He again told me, less gently, "Just do your best," and sent me back to hell.

Perhaps in response to my plea of being overwhelmed and underprepared, Director Johnson sent me to the National Academy of Corrections in Colorado for two- and four-week training sessions in leadership and management. There, my corrections education was expanded by interaction with professionals from across the country who were both the trainers and participants. In fact, this was such a great experience that I asked one instructor, "How can I become a trainer?" To my amazement, the response was, "Complete this application." And just when I thought I could not endure another day at Jackson, I received a letter from the academy offering me a two-year appointment. "Hurrah," I thought. "I'm getting out of prison!"

But when I called the director's office for a release date, my euphoria evaporated. "You can't go, sis," the director said. "Something's come up, but I can't talk about it right now."

So, I learned how a prisoner must feel when his parole is cancelled. Resentfully, I returned to Jackson. Only a month later, I found out that the "something" the director could not talk about was that I was to be named the first woman in Michigan to run a prison for men—the Michigan Dunes Correctional Facility in Holland.

In contrast to the breakneck pace of work at Jackson, I found that there were not many incidents at the Dunes, a medium-security prison. However, we did have a prisoner death: a nice man who had been the painter for the facility. Although it appeared to have been from natural causes, the prison doctor ordered an autopsy for confirmation. If staff had to observe these, I wanted to know what they would experience, so I tagged along with the prison physician. I recall the doctor who was performing the procedure looking at the prison doc and asking, "Is she going to be OK?" He replied, "I think so."

I realized the question had to do with my response to what was coming next. My background as a farm girl was helpful. I knew what the insides of pigs and cows looked like, and, to my amazement, a person was not much different. The smell of the skull bone as the cap was removed by the saw was disconcerting, but the rest of the process was just interesting. Today, many TV shows include more blood and body details than I saw that day, but in the early 1980s, only medical students were privy to the inner workings of a human body. I felt privileged to have been present when the natural death of the prisoner was confirmed.

While most staff seemed to be warming to my leadership style—which I described as "management by wandering around and listening"—one group still stymied me: the educators. One day, a group of them were approaching as we walked the main corridor; I smiled and greeted them. "How're you doing?"

Then I heard one say, after I had passed, "What do you think she meant by that?" That a smile and greeting would get such a response suggested trouble in paradise. As I talked with the school principal and his boss, the treatment director, I found that the teachers did not feel valued and that this had been the case since the prison opened. Also, I had initiated some changes in their area without consulting with them, which had increased their sense of alienation.

Since the budget had some room for it, I scheduled a three-day retreat at a local college where, through a series of assessments and exercises, we learned new ways to look at the conflicts we had experienced. I learned that offering staff a role in desired changes, and working though their concerns, allowed changes to be owned by everyone involved. We left the retreat with a better attitude toward our work together. After the retreat, one teacher initiated a mock interview session using community volunteers in the role of prospective employers of prisoner interviewees that proved to be a success.

»»»»»»»»»»»»»

After three-and-a-half years at the Dunes, Director Brown, who had succeeded Perry Johnson, named me warden at the Michigan Reformatory. This was another first-woman opportunity, as no female had led one of the old penitentiaries. He continued to find training opportunities for me and others who were experiencing rapid promotions. The Wharton School in Philadelphia offered a weeklong program for wardens from all over the country. One session in that leadership seminar was quite memorable. Participants were divided into four groups by gender and ethnicity—white men, white women, minority men, and minority women. Each group was asked to consider four questions. What was it like to be a member of their own group working in corrections and what was it like to be a member of each of the other three? Each group would then report to the others the result of their discussions.

Each group went into a private space and three of the four followed the directions. Unfortunately for them, the white males got so caught up in discussing what it was like to be white men working in corrections that they ran out of time to consider the ramifications for others. They reported, "It was about the same for everyone else." Since the other groups had said that they perceived significant differences for the various groups, the white males' report was not well received. The white men received quite direct feedback. "Your approach to this task," they were told, "reflects your lack of sensitivity about what it is like to be a minority of any type in the corrections business."

The other groups were unanimous in their perception that the role of the minority female was hardest. White women thought it was harder for them than for minority men, and minority men thought just the opposite. A white male warden from Michigan later told me, "I tried to get them on task because I knew what would happen when we reconvened." I do think some of the white guys got a wake-up call about gender and racial differences in the workplace.

At this point in my career, I had taken charge of finding the kind of education and training I thought would round out my development. In addition to conferences offered by the Michigan Corrections Association, I attended those put on by the American Correctional Association and North American Association of Warden and Superintendents. Another favorite gathering was the biennial Women Working in Corrections and Juvenile Justice conference. In 1995, I went to one in Pittsburgh. Because Michigan Corrections had developed a strong cadre of women, many in leadership positions, I thought my home state would be a good site for the next gathering in the fall of 1996.

Before confirming, though, I made sure Luella Burke would agree to co-chair. Finally, I called the Amway Grand Plaza Hotel in Grand Rapids and booked the conference for October 13-16, 1996, using my personal credit card. All the networking I had done paid off when the Women Police of Michigan, the Michigan Corrections Association, and the Michigan Sheriffs Association agreed to join the Department of Corrections as sponsors. We had over eight hundred attendees and made a profit of $40,000, which was shared between Nebraska, the conference's 1998 location, and the Department of Corrections, for scholarships for staff to attend the next conference. I had learned how to provide—with a lot of help—a successful national conference for women in the corrections profession!

After the conference, the mailroom supervisor came to me and said, "You are probably going to kill me, but I met someone who offered me a job in Florida." And I had to congratulate her, because that was just the sort of thing networking at conferences is about. Her husband also worked at the Reformatory and was retiring, so they both went happily off to the Sunshine State.

But women in corrections were not the only professionals who interested me. Wardens also had a special place in my heart, and I was excited to be tapped to go to Texas later in 1998 for warden peer-interaction training. This was an initiative by Sam Houston State University and involved wardens from around the country. The Texas DOC supported the training by permitting visits to their prisons, including an execution site. I loved the training. Wardens were asked to present what they regarded as a best practice from their agency—I described cognitive work with prisoners. Presentations were followed by questions and suggestions from peers. It was a great opportunity to share ideas and strategies and learn from each other. On the other hand, the practices in the Texas prisons seemed archaic, and I was horrified that they were proud of the efficiency offered by side-by-side electric chairs. Michigan, as a state, has never had the death penalty. I knew it was expensive to administer and research suggested it was ineffective as a deterrent. My conversations with wardens who had presided over executions also convinced me there was a human toll for prison workers who were involved in the taking of another's life, even if it was done under the color of law.

»»»»»»»»»»»

Looking back, I recognize how fortunate I was to have had Perry Johnson's hand guiding my initial career. In the years after he successfully introduced women to Michigan Corrections, he wrote an article describing his plan to identify about a dozen promising women and promote them aggressively, jump-starting their careers and ensuring that there was a cadre of strong and principled women leaders in the department. Although I was not aware of his plan, I did feel that responsibility. As I made decisions, I felt Perry was looking over my shoulder. As a result, I tried to be sure my performance would be up to his standards. Although there were no women as role models, the awareness that Perry was counting on me to succeed so that other women could follow kept me motivated, even during trying times.

And there you have it. That is how an Indiana farm girl who wanted to be an English teacher came to be a prison warden who, at the end of her career, was named Warden of the Year by the North American Association of Wardens and Superintendents, inducted into the Michigan Women's Hall of Fame, and received honorary doctorates from Grand Valley and Ferris State Universities for introducing cognitive work with prisoners to the Michigan Department of Corrections. Not bad for a welfare mother who just wanted a job.

2. PRISONS I HAVE KNOWN

Just like individuals, every prison has its own personality. It has been shaped by history, those who have lived and worked there, the leaders of that facility, and the agency that oversees operations. This might be a good time to mention that I have always thought of a prison as a small town, with all the services one might expect to find there. Most staff are responsible for security and operate like a police force. In fact, some prisoners call them "the PO-lice." There are other staff who provide essential services for prisoners—food, laundry, quartermaster, maintenance, transportation, library/law library, school, chapel, counseling, health care, barber shop, store, warehouse, and even a jail within the walls or fences. In addition, the administrative services, business, offender records, personnel, and maintenance departments, and additional warehouse space are outside the security perimeter.

Except for security, prisoners perform most of the work for prisons. Although staff oversee food service, prisoners make the food, serve it, and perform cleanup chores. Prisoner clerks assist with the library, school, chapel, and quartermaster functions. When I was a warden, a barber in the free world in Michigan could not get a license with a felony background, yet prisoners cut hair in institutions. They also clean, mow, shovel snow, and make repairs with staff supervision. Staff costs are a prison's largest part of the budget. Prisoner wages during my tenure were under a dollar a day for most jobs. Their labor saved the taxpayers a lot of money.

A common misperception is that staff carry a weapon inside a prison. The fact is that the primary tool used by staff is their brain. Prisoners have twenty-four hours a day to dream up ways to beat the systems we have developed, and staff must stay on their toes to prevent and detect rule violations, especially escapes or disturbances. Most disciplinary matters are handled internally; however, felonies committed in Michigan's prisons are referred to the state police, with prosecutions handled by the county. An arsenal contains restraints, rifles, shotguns, handguns, and chemical agents. These are assigned to perimeter and prisoner transport vehicles, and used during annual weapons qualifications and for riot training. Fortunately, I never had to order them to be used for a disturbance.

And just like a small town, the mayor (warden) can be ousted if the citizens (staff and/or prisoners) become unhappy with that mayor. I sometimes say, "Think of prison operations as a three-legged stool. One leg represents prisoners, one leg represents staff and internal operations, and the third leg represents external forces—Central Office, the community, prisoners' families and friends, the legislature, and the courts. If any of those legs get out of balance, the prison won't run right, and the warden will eventually have to go."

»»»»»»»»»»»»»

I loved the prison headquarters for the camps. "Well, this looks like the fishing camp we went to on vacation when I was a kid," I thought when I saw the building for the first time. Camp Brighton, where I was the camp supervisor, also had the vibe of a summer camp. The outdoor visiting area even hosted family picnics on Sundays, weather permitting. Prisoners lived in long, open dormitories lined with bunks. They ate in a communal dining hall and played ball and tennis in the summer and basketball in the gym in the winter. And the rural setting could only be called bucolic.

And then there was Jackson. Formally known as the State Prison of Southern Michigan, it had been built in the 1930s and was the world's largest walled prison. That size made management difficult, and it was divided into three parts when I worked there. Minimum-custody prisoners lived in Trustee Division in the South cellblocks or on farms that were much like the camps. Medium-custody inmates were in cellblocks and modular units on the north side of the prison. And the part where I worked, Central Complex, housed the worst of the bunch, all in concrete and steel cellblocks. There were seven of these, all five tiers high. Some had back-to-back cells with a utility catwalk in between. Others had the cells around the outside of the block, with an open central area. All smelled of male sweat and fear.

While two of the units in Central Complex were honor blocks, for men who had jobs and clear conduct records, two others were for management problems who needed to be segregated or for prisoners needing protection. Those remaining were general-population high security. Walking the narrow catwalks next to the open bars was always a risk. "Will anyone dress me out?" was always my concern. Getting dressed out included being doused with water, urine, or worse. Fortunately, that never happened to me. There were other parts of Jackson, but as the housing deputy I was responsible only for the cellblocks.

When I escaped to head the Dunes, it was like going home to Camp Brighton, except it was an upscale version. The Dunes was originally a Catholic seminary. The students had lived in open dorms and that was where most of the prisoners lived. Instructors and administrators had single rooms or lived three to a spacious room. We used those accommodations for honor units and that gave the inmates in the dorms hope for better housing. One warden told me, "You probably have the only joint in the country with marble mopboards." And the building was lovely. The exterior was stone, with a huge stone cross and other sacramental sculptures. Inside the gates there was a long curved hallway, with lots of windows flooding the classrooms with light, and a dining room like the prow of a ship facing the dune that gave the prison its name. The dune also blocked the view of Lake Michigan. This medium-custody prison was just one step up from minimum security and was a dream to run. One time the night shift commander proudly announced, "We have gone a whole year without anyone calling in sick." Staff were dedicated and professional.

There were just over four hundred prisoners and nearly that many volunteers. The Christian Reformed churches of Holland took seriously the biblical admonition to visit those in prison, and we were happy to use their time and energy. When the Catholic Church gave the seminary to the Department of Corrections, it included enough land to provide what became the Saugatuck Dunes State Park, so we had that adjacent to the facility. There had been a convent in a mansion on the property, so that was where the state police established their post. I'm happy to say we didn't give them much business, but the lieutenant there let me roam around the lovely Felt Mansion, which had a widow's walk from which the lake was visible. Today the mansion has been restored to its former glory and is open for tours and events.

After three and a half years at the Dunes, I was named warden of the Michigan Reformatory in Ionia. I had never set foot in that prison before my appointment. I knew it was the oldest in the system, with parts dating to 1877, but did not know how run-down it had become. Because it was slated for closure, routine maintenance had been deferred; there were trees growing on some roofs!

As a result of the 1981 riot, we were under a federal consent decree. That court order required attention to prisoners' out-of-cell time, classification (which combines security level placement with program requirements), sanitation, protection from harm, and many physical plant changes, primarily related to fire safety. I recall the business manager, Paul Renico, and I conferring.

"Is there some way we can get some of our urgent maintenance projects to be part of the consent decree so we can get money to fix them?" I asked.

And Paul was creative in some of his funding requests. Over time we got the place cleaned up and fixed up, but even though it had been five years since a riot had destroyed the school and damaged other areas, the psychic wounds of that event weighed on staff.

"Blood on the floor every day," was how my boss Dan Bolden described the climate at the Reformatory. We housed the high-security young offenders for the Department of Corrections, and a culture of violence was a point of pride for the staff. "The Gladiator School" was what some called the place, and I was determined to change that.

"Excessive use of force will not be tolerated," I told shift command. And then I backed it up by firing or disciplining staff who used retaliatory violence. When I reviewed the mix of segregation and protection cells, it seemed to me we needed more of the former so we could have fewer of the latter. As the consent decree was implemented, my wish for more space to keep violent prisoners out of the general population was granted. And not surprisingly, the number of prisoners asking for protection went down as the predators were kept in our jail within the prison.

One huge plus at the Reformatory was two Michigan State Industry operations—an industrial laundry that served multiple prisons and a furniture factory that provided wood furniture for many state offices. Both were huge multistory brick buildings, which presented security risks—the laundry with toxic cleaning products, hot presses, and frequent trips through the vehicle sally port, and the furniture factory with the tools and materials related to manufacturing. However, the well-paid and plentiful jobs for prisoners more than made up for those concerns.

Because of the young population, we also had a large school with dedicated teachers that included special education and vocational trade training. With consent decree funds, we converted an underused auditorium to a gym and added program spaces for counseling and cognitive activities. A chapel offered Christian and Islamic services and a large yard permitted organized sports as well as individual exercise.

For security, there was a forbidding wall, along one side of which ran the aptly named Wall Street. Along another wall, as a testament to the prison's central role in Ionia's history, was Main Street. Gun towers reinforced the wall's security. Across Wall Street was a minimum-security dorm that operated much like Camp Brighton and provided workers for the maintenance building, the warehouse, the power plant, and the training house. A derelict house sat across from my office—it had been the warden's home it its glory days. Wardens no longer lived onsite and the home had fallen into disrepair. I was sad to see it torn down, but it had no use, was too expensive to maintain, and we needed the parking space, so it had to go.

Although Camp Brighton was where I cut my teeth as a supervisor, and the Dunes was undoubtedly the most beautiful prison in the most idyllic setting

I had worked in, my heart will always be with the Reformatory. The young prisoners, many serving life with no possibility for parole, had so many needs, and most staff were patient and decent when dealing with them. Over time, we were no longer a gladiator school and could host visitors without concern for their safety. Staff learned to be proud of the programming offered as well as the security provided by running a humane facility.

3. OFFENDER PROGRAMS: CHANGING HEARTS AND MINDS

Traditional prisoner programs include routine work, education, religious services, recreation, hobbycraft, and a library, including law library services. These are directed from Central Office, but there are sometimes opportunities for creating new prisoner activities.

My first local initiative was at Camp Brighton. I was talking with a pastor who provided Protestant services at the camp. We had both noticed the "poor me" attitude many Brighton prisoners displayed. Even though they were robbers, burglars, drunk drivers, and occasionally murderers, almost all characterized their activities as something they had to do, and saw their apprehension and incarceration as a wrong imposed upon them by society.

A robber who had killed a husband and wife said, "We just wanted the money. If he had not fought back, we would not have had to kill him, and if she had not tried to save her husband, we would not have had to hurt her." It was the victims' fault that they had died and put the poor prisoner away for all these years. If they had just given them what they wanted, the robbers would have gone away without anyone being harmed. "After all," the prisoner reasoned, "insurance covers stolen stuff, so that does not count as harm."

I asked the pastor, "Any suggestions on how to get my guys past this kind of thinking?"

He said, "My church members volunteer at Hillcrest. They need volunteers desperately. I'll bet they'd even take prisoners." Hillcrest was a mental health facility about fifteen minutes from the camp that housed severely handicapped and developmentally disabled young people.

As you might guess, my security-minded staff did not think this was a good idea at all. These were the objections I heard: "There are female staff who might be accosted." "Someone must transport prisoners and we can't spare the staff, plus it is a security risk to put prisoners on the road after dark." "Nobody has done that before, so it is probably just a bad idea."

These comments helped me develop the arguments needed to sell the idea. I told my boss, "We want to conduct a pilot project at Hillcrest Center for ninety days to see if it improves prisoner behavior. I will work from noon until eight-thirty and transport the prisoners, leaving all assigned staff at the facility. We'll start with fifteen prisoners, going out in groups of five each week."

He said, "Go ahead and give it a try." Interestingly, he never asked about the program, which continued well beyond the pilot's ninety days.

We helped Hillcrest residents bounce on trampolines, go sledding, make snowmen, create craft items, and make and eat ice-cream sundaes. It was interesting to me to see a macho prisoner tenderly wipe the face of an ice-cream-covered resident or bounce with and smile encouragingly at a resident on the trampoline. The best times were the return to the camp. In the dark of the van, I heard one man say, "Those kids don't have a chance at life. I will get a fresh start when I get out." There were variations on this theme, but, as the pastor and I had hoped, their time as volunteers helped this group of prisoners move from their victim attitude to one aware of possibilities.

On no occasion did I hear a complaint about any prisoner's behavior. In fact, when the time for the Special Olympics competition in Howell came, a Hillcrest supervisor asked, "Any chance all fifteen participants can help? It would let us take more residents." This idea was both wonderful and terrifying.

I remember thinking, "I can't supervise fifteen prisoners myself. I'll have to ask staff to volunteer to change days off and schedules so we will have enough coverage to run the camp as well as transport and supervise the prisoners at Howell High School." To my delight, that part went smoothly.

Another element to address was the unpredictability of offender behavior. While there had been no problems so far, this event was to be held on a spring day, when many scantily dressed young women volunteers would be present. And, to add to my concern, Howell was Michigan's center for the Ku Klux Klan. There were several Black prisoners in my volunteer group, and I was more worried about citizens' reactions to them than any behavior the offenders might demonstrate. But I could only deal with what was under my control, so I spoke to the prisoner volunteers. "OK, guys, we have a chance to help Hillcrest take residents to the Special Olympics. Some people think you'll get distracted by local volunteers, especially the young ladies. If the program is to continue, you all need to be on your best behavior."

Fortunately—for the program and me—the day went well. Each offender stayed with his assigned resident, no incidents were reported, and everyone returned to camp at the end of the day. In fact, Hillcrest valued this program so highly that when I was promoted, they trained one of their staff to supervise offenders; he transported the prisoner volunteers until Hillcrest closed.

While Jackson's post-riot climate didn't support additional programs, when I got to the Dunes, I started stretching the definition of prisoner programs. One of the traditions in my family was to bake cookies and make candy during the Christmas holiday to give to friends and teachers. Because holidays in prison are so sad, I decided to invite prisoners who did not get many visits to help me bake cookies and serve them to the prisoner population at a candlelight reception. I even told shift command, "For this event, food can be taken out of the dining room." I had to grin when prisoners left with cookies stuffed into their shirts. A few staff joined me as bakers the first year and more came to help when we repeated the event.

Another Dunes activity was Warden's Appreciation Day. That was an end-of-summer celebration dependent on having a "good" summer. We defined that as no disruptions on the yard or in the units. Since the riots at the major penitentiaries in May 1981, staff worried about another round of prisoner uprisings. The Prisoner Benefit Fund paid for the ice cream and hot dogs, and staff were the servers. That role reversal was much appreciated by the inmates. One year, we even had donkey softball—a variation on traditional softball where the participants, after a hit or walk, had to move to the next base with their assigned (live, miniature) donkey. Hilarity ensued when the uncooperative donkeys bucked, kicked, and broke loose. Some of the stronger prisoners even picked up their donkey and strode to their base. Who says there is no fun to be had in prison?

»»»»»»»»»»»

One of my favorite new programs for the Reformatory, "Prisoners Who Care, Read," was the brainchild of literacy volunteer Mary Ann Hagermeyer. She had been working with low-level readers and wanted to find a way to reward them for reaching literacy goals. She got funding to purchase children's books that prisoners read and recorded. The books and recordings were then mailed or given to the offenders' children during a visit. What a great way to encourage reading and model good parenting. I was happy to partner with her on that effort.

Many of the Reformatory's young prisoners needed to complete high school. When we installed cable TV, prisoners who earned their GED had the option of saying a few words for a recording to be played for their fellow inmates. I think they enjoyed showing off their caps and gowns while offering encouragement to others.

»»»»»»»»»»»

When I took the helm at the Reformatory, the first order of business was to get the place cleaned up and under control. It was six years before I started to look for something to add to traditional programs. What still fascinated me was prisoners' attitudes and thinking. Coincidentally, the National Academy of Corrections, which had already provided so much helpful training, offered a new course called "Cognitive Approaches to Changing Inmate Behaviors." Well, the behavior of my young violent prisoners needed changing, so I asked staff, "Anyone interested in going to Colorado to learn about cognitive programs for prisoners?"

To my delight, Psychologist Jim Conklin, Unit Manager Mark Gassman, and Counselor Dave Zarka volunteered to join me in 1992 for this training. It offered information on three cognitive avenues that research had shown changed prisoner conduct. The one we came away from the session planning to use was called "Skill Training." The premise was that practicing new skills, ones that a prisoner identified as desiring, would lead to changes in that prisoner's thinking, with the result that the prisoner would be less likely to reoffend. The other possibilities were "Problem Solving" and "Cognitive Restructuring." Even though I had heard staff say that a first-degree murderer was just a really bad problem solver, we had rejected "Problem Solving" as not being broad enough to impact the young men housed at the Reformatory. We thought "Cognitive Restructuring" would take too long and was too complicated and decided we did not have the time or resources to tackle that option.

As we planned for implementation, one of us had a lightbulb moment— "The violent young men we have really need cognitive restructuring." Many prisoners saw themselves as victims, even though they had raped, robbed, or killed. When asked what their plans were after release, most said, "I will start my own business." This was stated with conviction even though many had not even graduated high school and came from impoverished backgrounds. They would describe themselves as good people despite histories of violent crimes.

I asked myself, "How in the world will we implement a cognitive restructuring program?" I knew Jack Bush and Brian Billodeau ran a violent offender program in the Vermont Department of Corrections. While planning a vacation I asked my husband, "Could we go to Vermont and visit their program?" He agreed to put it on our itinerary and I was quite impressed with what I saw.

"Can I send a team from the Reformatory to observe your program?" I asked. Jack and Brian were welcoming. The Reformatory team visited and was ready to try a similar program on their return, but we still had to figure out how to structure our program. My next move was to ask the National Institute of Corrections to fund a seminar so Reformatory staff could hear from Bush and Billodeau in Michigan. When the request was granted, we learned about cognitive theory as well as barriers offenders would raise and the interventions to counteract them.

There were prison staff, mostly mental health professionals, who thought officers and counselors did not have the educational background to provide this kind of programming. Access to counseling from the few psychologists at the facility was reserved for those nearing release or in acute crisis, so I told the naysayers, "I do not see how the earnest involvement of staff trained in cognitive work could be harmful. The prisoners in the program are all volunteers and staff have been cautioned to send anyone who seems to be mentally ill to see you guys." This seemed to mollify the mental health practitioners, but most of them never offered support for the staff doing cognitive work.

We named the program "Strategies for Thinking Productively" (STP). Prisoners with violent crimes were given priority for inclusion. Phase I involved fourteen lessons delivered in sixteen sessions over an eight-week period. The DOC agreed this would qualify as group counseling, so offenders were happy to participate. Those who wished to continue into Phase II had to agree to stay at the Reformatory for up to two years. For those wishing to continue to consolidate the changes they had begun in Phase II, Phase III was available.

The premise of all cognitive programs is: "How you think controls how you behave." In cognitive restructuring, prisoners identify behavior they want to change and then determine the attitudes and beliefs that support that behavior. Several mechanisms can be used for behavior change, including thought stopping, but the most enduring is the replacement of old attitudes and beliefs with new ones.

In 1994, we were able to house Phase II men together. Program participants told us, "Living with other men trying to do the hard work of self-change is helpful." Phase II involved group meetings of up to eight prisoners with two staff as observers. Each group was structured around a thinking report of a single prisoner and lasted about an hour. The featured prisoner presented a situation that got him into trouble and all the thoughts and feelings he could recall during the event. He also noted the attitudes and beliefs he identified as supporting the thinking. His fellow prisoners then asked him questions to help him clarify or find additional thoughts and feelings. Sometimes they suggested he identify additional beliefs or attitudes he had not considered. The presenting prisoner was always the final arbiter, though, about the thinking report's contents. Staff were there to keep order, keep the questioning respectful and on target, and, in the long term, to determine whether the prisoners were doing the hard work of self-change and assisting others toward that goal.

For program integrity, groups were periodically audited. I had the privilege of auditing when one prisoner had his lightbulb moment. "I like to hurt people," he said. I wish I could describe his tone—it seemed to contain revulsion, self-knowledge, and wonder. That epiphany spurred him to read everything we had in the program library and to redouble his efforts at change. While his current crime was nonviolent, one of his previous crimes was directing the sexual assault of another prisoner in the county jail.

To move from Phase II to Phase III, prisoners had to offer a thinking report on their crime. Through thinking reports and journal activity, this prisoner also recalled being sexually assaulted by an uncle as a youngster. (This prompted a referral to the mental health team.) This prisoner could have chosen his nonviolent current offense, but instead presented about the sexual assault. When staff asked him why he made that choice, he responded, "This is the behavior I most want to change."

We were clear that he liked to hurt people. He had what looked like marbles at the joint of his jaws because he so often clenched his teeth to avoid hitting someone. Most staff stayed a clear arm's length away from him because we knew what a short fuse he had. It was unusual for him to be out of segregation for longer than a few months because of his explosive temper. While in the program, he managed to avoid violent misconduct and was able to move to reduced custody at another prison. I have always thought of him as the offender who accomplished the most significant change while in the program.

An additional element of Phase II was journaling. Each prisoner was charged with keeping track of his daily efforts to change and to review the journal with a staff partner weekly. This was complicated by some offenders near illiteracy, but those who wanted to be in the program had to find a way to handle all the requirements. From a security perspective, journaling was the most troubling. While we wanted prisoners to have privacy for what could be difficult discussions, we needed to be able to see that staff members were safe during those meetings. Most offices we used had windows and were well lighted.

Only on one occasion was a staff person at risk, and the prisoner involved had absorbed enough of the program's goals that he confessed his intentions before carrying out his plan. He had chosen a non-custody staff member who worked in the mail room. She had excellent instincts for delivering STP, but did not work inside the secure perimeter except when working with STP prisoners. To execute his plan he had managed to put together a kit designed to immobilize his journal partner. It included a strip of braided sheet to bind her, another piece of cloth for a gag, and a cord from a laundry bag to use as a garrote. He had planned a murder/suicide based on a movie he had watched. Over time, he had developed feelings for this staff member. He understood that she did not return these feelings, but had decided if he could not have her, no one else would either. No one had detected his inappropriate attraction and it was only his confession that averted a tragedy. I counted it as a win for the program, but the prisoner had to go to maximum security with relevant misconduct reports, even though he had done the right thing by letting staff know his plan.

One fun event connected with STP occurred when John Bergman with the Geese Theatre Company came to the Reformatory to teach us to use role-playing in group work. I signed a manifest to allow Tosser, John's small, curly-haired white dog, to go to the chapel for training. While some offenders seemed leery of the animal, others were excited to pet and hold it. Therapy animals in prisons were not yet common, but I could see where these might be useful. While some prisoners were involved in scenarios, others took turns caring for Tosser. I recall one man starting rough play; he was admonished by his peers to be gentle with the pup.

By June 1996, there were eight Phase I STP groups inside the facility and two at the dorm. Five Phase II groups were operating in the old Adjustment Center, now called G-Block. By January 1997, two prisoners had moved into Phase III, with two waiting to be interviewed to make that move. It was not until the fall of 1997 that five prisoners were in Phase III. That was the maximum number in that status. The primary reason was that prisoners' positive conduct while in the program resulted in their eligibility for reduced custody. We encouraged men to move on when they had completed Phase II and were eligible to step down in custody level. Not only was that a good test of their commitment to change, but it also freed space at the Reformatory for prisoners who needed the structure and security we provided.

For those who did stay for Phase III, we provided journal partners and socializing activities. One I initiated was a weekly warden's dinner. I brought in silverware, plates, glasses, and even cloth placemats and napkins. Up to eight individuals were able to dine at a time, so I invited staff involved in STP, and sometimes staff critical of the program, to join us in a group room near G-Block. We began the meal, which was the same food being served in the chow hall, with a moment of silence. Then serving bowls and platters were passed and conversation ensued. Afterward, the prisoners did the dishes while I counted and locked up the silverware, plates, and glasses. When queried about the need to learn about place settings and the niceties of dining, I responded, "When you are released and take a young lady out to dinner, you need to know this stuff."

Because most seemed unfamiliar with dining family style, I asked about that. One guy responded, "Sitting around a table to eat is not what we do. When I was hungry, Moms gave me money and I went down to the corner." Others agreed.

Even though research into cognitive programs has confirmed their efficacy, I wrote to colleges and universities within driving distance of the Reformatory and solicited researchers to validate our version. Dr. Agnes Baro of Grand Valley

State University agreed to conduct research on the STP program. Because of the voluntary nature of STP, we identified prisoners for a control group from other self-help programs such as AA/NA, religious groups, or school. The researchers selected a random group from this pool. Dr. Baro looked at the behavior of both Phase I and Phase II participants as compared to the controls, all of whom had been in programs at least eight weeks. To my surprise, Phase I prisoners showed a statistically significant reduction in disobeying a direct order (DDO) misconducts. In Phase II, the reduction in DDO continued and there was also a statistically significant reduction in misconduct for assault. Since DDO was the most frequently occurring misconduct in all prisons in Michigan, a reduction was important. Also, DDO events sometimes escalate into more serious misconduct. I think anyone would agree that fewer assaults in prison is also desirable. In the case of prisoners serving a term of years, the timekeeping system automatically added a week to the offender's sentence for every month in which a misconduct occurred. Reduction in misconduct translated to earlier eligibility for parole, which could mean a savings for the taxpayer. We celebrated the good news brought by Dr. Baro's research.

While STP was voluntary, I was curious about how cognitive restructuring might work if it was mandated. We were having trouble meeting an element of a federal consent decree related to adequate out-of-cell time. I suggested we merge consent decree requirements and STP efforts by developing a not-voluntary cognitive program. The research told us that men who sought to change improved in two key misconduct areas. We wanted to know whether compelled cognitive exposure could also have a positive effect on conduct. Director McGinnis agreed that prisoners who screened Level V (maximum security) could be assigned to the program, even if that required transfer to the Reformatory. Ferris State University agreed to conduct the research this time. The legislature funded additional officer and case manager positions so that we could expand the number of groups and journal partners.

To differentiate this program from STP, we brainstormed and came up with the moniker CHANGE, the acronym standing for "Cognitive Housing Approach: New Goals Environment." Once staff and physical plant improvements were in place, we began moving prisoners into the program.

In discussing the research design with the Ferris team, we decided on a pre/post evaluation. In other words, we would look at the prisoners' behavior for a period before program participation and then again for the same period after completion. One element I stressed to the Ferris team was a research structure that would permit individual prisoner behavior to be the key. I anticipated that a few inmates would simply refuse to participate, each receiving a DDO misconduct daily, and did not want the behavior of a knucklehead or two to be aggregated with what we hoped would be improved conduct for most. The research team split their duties so that two came to the facility to monitor group sessions and documentation while the third crunched the numbers.

Not surprisingly, prisoners selected for the CHANGE program were hostile. They resisted moving to a different cell or coming to the Reformatory. All needed to complete their GED (high school equivalency), so were assigned to school, and most went to that program willingly. Attending groups for cognitive work was a different story. Staff got high marks for their ability to persuade most to give it a try.

An offender I recall talking with was typical. He had been in and out of segregation for fighting and assault and was reluctant to cooperate with staff. I told him what we told prisoners involved with cognitive work: "You have three choices in life: change, stay the same, or die. I trust you don't want the last option. You know what to expect if you stay the same. The CHANGE program offers a third path. You might give it a try." He didn't have a comeback to that, but staff told me he came to the group. It took awhile, but he finally began to participate; housing officers reported his attitude in the unit also improved.

A new manual that combined problem solving, skill training, and restructuring was used for CHANGE. For the skill-training lessons, prisoners were given small blue cards with the steps of the skill listed. Staff reported that for skills like "asking a question" or "having a difficult conversation," they would observe prisoners consulting their cards before engaging. It is hard to imagine needing cue cards for these basic skills, but if your way of getting what you want has been violence or the threat of violence, you probably did not develop the skills most pro-social people take for granted. CHANGE staff felt prisoners were adapting to the program and many were making positive changes. We waited for the Ferris research to confirm that belief.

However, when Ferris presented their preliminary evaluation, it was not good. Their report suggested that participation was not only failing to result in improved conduct, it was harming prisoners by creating more misconduct, which could have resulted in a prisoner's being transferred to maximum security. Even though this information conflicted with staff reports of participants' increased self-control and attempts at change, I elected to believe the numbers. I contacted the director and said, "Ferris says we're harming prisoners with CHANGE. I suggest we end the program." He agreed.

Several years after I had retired, I spotted an article in Corrections Today, the American Correctional Association's magazine, which claimed the program was a success. It did not name the Reformatory (citing a Midwestern prison), but the author was the numbers cruncher from Ferris. The program's description made it clear it was about CHANGE. Although I was angry and upset when I saw the article, I did not contact the author. Either he lied to us initially or fudged the numbers when cognitive work became more common and acceptable. It made no difference at that point because the program no longer existed.

While research confirms that traditional academic and vocational programs have a positive effect on recidivism, I am heartened to know that cognitive programming has spread throughout the Department of Corrections and is now one of the traditional prisoner programs. Perhaps it is a coincidence that Michigan has been able to close prisons and reduce the population from just over fifty thousand to under thirty-five thousand. I like to think that the expansion of cognitive programming has played a part in the lower number of incarcerated men and women.

4. ONE PRISONER'S STORY OF CHANGE

Ron Hammond committed a cold-blooded murder when he was seventeen years old. He and a friend hijacked a car and forced the young driver out at gunpoint. Ron ordered the driver into the trunk and, when he refused, told him, "I am going to count to three. If you are not in the trunk when I get to three, I will shoot you." The driver did not get in the trunk. Ron shot the man in the head, killing him.

I met Mr. Hammond at the Michigan Reformatory in 1996 after we had started the STP cognitive restructuring program. He volunteered to participate and worked his way through the initial phases. When it was time for him to have a journal partner, I volunteered. I had audited groups where he had presented and felt he was saying all the right things, but not taking them to heart. I told staff, "Hammond is a bright guy and I think he will be a challenging journal partner. Let me work with him."

Part of cognitive work is to identify behavior you want to change and develop strategies for implementing the changes. Mr. Hammond had identified six target behaviors, starting with pride—refusing to admit a wrong decision, and continuing with verbal abuse, physical aggression, refusal to listen, dehumanizing, and retaliation. These are very common traits for men who have committed crimes and matched what I had seen from Mr. Hammond's conduct.

When we started meeting, he was curious. "Why are you my journal partner?" he asked.

"I thought you'd be a challenge," I answered honestly. Although we did the work called for in the cognitive program, he took our time together to pick my brain on issues of crime and punishment.

"I'm a lifer. What good can this program do me if I'll never get out of prison?" he queried.

My response was the same I gave all men who asked about cognitive work:

"You will have a life whether in prison or out. This work gives you a chance to have the best possible experience. And the pendulum of public attitudes swings. Right now, it is all about punishment, but a time may come when you'll have more chances than you have today and you need to be ready if that time comes."

During journal sessions, Mr. Hammond developed what he called his prescription for his own life. "First thing is to accept my punishment. As long as I am alive, I can have a life. I deserve some type of happiness. It is time I stop walking through life in a fog and live. I may fall; I may make mistakes, but they will be mine." These statements became a blueprint for a change in attitude.

As Mr. Hammond became eligible for reduced security, he was reluctant to leave. He finally decided to move on and wrote to me:

There were two specific things that brought me to the conclusion that it is time to consider going to a lower custody. The first was that I have worked hard to change the way I think and act. I have done well here since I came back from Marquette in the summer of 1993. I have stayed pretty much ticket free, maintained a good work record and have done my best to change for the better. I feel that it is time to give myself a little credit for the work I have done. To give myself a chance at what little happiness I may obtain under the condition of my confinement.

He continued:

The second is that I can not obtain that here at the Michigan Reformatory. I don't feel that the attitudes and beliefs of the individuals I live among here are conducive to that goal. I do not feel as if I am superior to them in anyway [sic]. Only that they are at a phase in their lives that I have already passed through. Through growing older, STP and just life's experiences within prison I can no longer rationalize the actions and lifestyles of those around me. Even though there will be those who hold the same beliefs and lifestyles that the majority do here, in any prison. I don't feel there will be as many. There will be more opportunity for me to come up from underground and be more social, to build a life, to find some kind of balance. Right now I am finding it hard to stay focused on my goal and I am having more negative thoughts than positive. There for [sic] I have decided that it is time to leave. To go someplace where I can settle in and do the remainder of my sentence, however long that may be.

Not long after that communication, Mr. Hammond transferred to lower custody. I should note that he lived alone in a cell at the Reformatory. In lower custody, he lived in an open dormitory setting with no private space. He wrote to me again:

The first few weeks here, for me, can only be described as pure hell. Everyone is so sociable. Which did not sit well with my like 'to be left alone.' I am doing much better at it now though. I still don't care too much for being around people allot [sic]. But I am learning ways of getting along with them without going into one of my cycles.

(A cycle is a way of thinking that leads to actions that gets a person into trouble.) He continued:

But overall, I think I have adjusted well. The open bay setting was not even half as bad as I thought it would be. All the movement drove me nuts for a week or so. But I got used to that too. The only serious problem I have had is not having my job. Not having that challenge and financial independence has at times made this place unbearable. Even now it cases [sic] me to wonder if I made the right choice.

Then I did not hear from Mr. Hammond for an extended period. His next letter said:

I am writing to once again thank you for giving me the opportunity to acquire the necessary tools for change. Also, I am writing to ask if any other institution, besides the Michigan Reformatory, has started a STP Phase III group yet. I wish I could tell you that, in the almost two years I have been gone from the Michigan Reformatory, things have gone well. But, that is not the case. Things have not been easy, I've had relapses, and trouble finding a comfort zone almost from the start. My biggest relapse and the start of my backwards slide, was not being able to accept that I could not support myself. My pride got the best of me. Even though we discussed this very issue during journal sessions prior to my leaving the Michigan Reformatory, I never imagined it would be this hard. Presently I am trying to halt the relapse. To stop the snowball effect and begin to regain some of the things I lost over the last twenty months. My relapse began when I could not support myself. I struggled with it for a few months. Then I relapsed back to hustling by dealing cards and making and selling wine. But making wine was even worse, as I am an alcoholic. So it was only a matter of time before I was drinking again. I received three substance abuse tickets (misconduct reports) in July of 1998. The day after I received the last substance abuse ticket I was placed on the call-out for an interview with MSI (Michigan State Industries, a well-paying job placement). Because of the substance abuse tickets I could not work in MSI. The snowball was now rolling downhill.

He went on to say he was transferred to an Upper Peninsula prison about a year later after several prisoners with a history of making wine were transferred out. Also, his visits were suspended, an action related to the substance abuse history.

As an aside, I will note that making wine, what prisoners called "spud juice," was simple. First, you steal yeast, fruit, and sugar from the kitchen. In a garbage bag, add water to your stolen items and stash the mixture under your bed or in your locker while it ferments. If you're in a hurry and it is winter, you can put the bag behind heater covers, but if the heater is in a common area, that risks loss of control over a valuable commodity. If the final option is selected, you must be prepared to retaliate if ripped off.

Later in the letter he related:
Since I've been here I've began [sic] to take small steps to get back control of myself. I know that any setback I have had, any punishment I have been given was deserved. In fact it was earned. As it all was a direct result of my own decisions. I also know that if it is going to turn back around it will have to be myself that turns it around.

He then described his involvement in substance abuse counseling and decision to learn to live frugally. He ended the letter with a request:
For a while I regretted leaving the Michigan Reformatory. But I no longer feel that way. Even though I have relapsed and things are hard, I know it was for the best. If I had never left I would of [sic] continued living with a false sense of change. But if I can truly make that change happen while facing my targeted behaviors everyday [sic] I will be far better off in the long run. If there is another STP Phase III group I would truly appreciate it if you would let me know where. I would like to approach my target behaviors like alcoholism. As a life long struggle. As I intend to continue attending AA after I complete Substance Abuse Counseling. I would also like to attend STP Phase III group. I think I can now truly appreciate the importance of the support that journaling and group provides... I felt disappointed in myself for awhile. Because I felt I let myself and everyone who helped me down. But I am starting to accept that failure as a growing process. To not continue to try would be failure. I've simply not had as easy of time of it as I had hoped I would. Eventually, though, if I work at it hard enough, I'll get it right.

I responded:
As far as I know, there is no STP Phase II in any level II prison...Jeff Angstman (a unit manager at Carson City) has participated in our training sessions and is quite knowledgeable in the area of cognitive work. I have talked with Warden Jones...and he is willing to have you placed in the multi-security...with the ultimate goal of moving to Level II in about 6 months providing your conduct is clear. He indicates you may be able to work out a journaling arrangement with RUM Angstman...I was sorry to hear of your unwise decisions but agree that you're making a responsible decision to get back into the program. Even if not placed at Carson City, you can journal independently and work on the thinking that has been getting you into trouble. Good luck.

Then I retired and thought I was unlikely to know what happened to Ron Hammond. I was shocked to receive a letter at my home in 2016. He was now at the Handlon Michigan Training Unit, a place that housed younger offenders.

Since he did not fit in the usual age range, I was interested in hearing how he had ended up at that prison.

His letter did not address that question. Instead he wrote:

Over the past 17 years I have often said you impacted my life more than anyone else. Had you not brought the STP program to the Michigan Reformatory, I may never have taken a serious look at how my thoughts and actions were the cause of all my troubles I [sic] life. Without the STP program I may still be blaming others.

He continued:

Not only did the program itself have a huge impact upon me, I also lean heavily upon conversations we had in our 1 on 1 journal sessions. Those conversations have been my bedrock for more than a decade and a half.

Later, he said:

I would hear your words and remember you telling me to always remember that views toward 'Crime and Punishment' swing like a pendulum, constantly moving from one extreme to the other. That one day in my lifetime that pendulum may swing in my favor. Even though that force that controls that pendulum is out of my control, how I choose to live my life isn't. I could either continue to make positive changes, to strive to do what is right and maybe one day have a chance to go home, or I could give up, surrender to my environment and guarantee that I would never go home.

Mr. Hammond went on to describe a promise he made to himself to become a better man and to someday thank me for my part in his change. Then, I said to myself, "Now he is getting to the real purpose of this letter," because he brought up a Supreme Court decision directing all states to review the records of offenders who had been given a life sentence for crimes they committed prior to age eighteen. I read on, expecting to find a request from this prisoner to support his quest for resentencing to a term of years, making him eligible for parole. That expectation reflected my own attitude about offenders—that they offer compliments before asking for a favor. I was wrong.

He ended the letter as follows:

I wanted to say Thank You. Some people take a job and do just what is required of them...you did the job in a manner that had a serious impact on my life and many others as well. Words alone cannot express how much your actions have meant to me, but I wanted you to know that your efforts were not wasted, they made a difference. Thank you.

And that was my last letter from Mr. Hammond for almost four years. I was not surprised, though, to hear from an attorney with the State Appellate Defender Office. Katherine Root contacted me to see if I would testify on behalf of Mr. Hammond for his resentencing hearing. My initial thought was reflexive: "No way." I had spent my entire career listening to prisoners who claimed they were in prison for crimes they did not commit or those who wanted a favorable recommendation for parole. My belief about the criminal justice system was simple. I had always thought, "Judges sentence; I incarcerate; I have no role in the question of guilt or innocence. Once someone is in my prison, my job is to keep him safe and work to make him a better citizen when released, period."

But Mr. Hammond was the only prisoner who had continued to keep me updated about his life in prison and his struggles to become a better person. Maybe it was time for me to question one of my core beliefs. So I told Ms. Root, "I have never supported a prisoner's quest for release; however, I will consider doing that for Mr. Hammond on one condition—that you arrange a meeting between him and me so I can question him directly about his current approach to life." She followed through and I met with Mr. Hammond at the Handlon Michigan Training Unit in the fall of 2019.

I'm not sure which of the three of us was the most nervous—Kathleen Root and Ron Hammond, both of whom needed me as a character witness for a life-altering hearing—or me. I was about to make a judgment critical to their mutual goal of getting Mr. Hammond's sentence changed to a term of years so he might someday be paroled. I had been out of the business of corrections for more than fifteen years; it felt odd to go through the security processes necessary to get to the attorney visiting room just inside the main gates. Ron Hammond joined us with a folder of materials and quiet determination. When I had last seen Ron, he was a slender young man, full of bravado and sure he could con his warden. The man I met that fall day was graying and showed evidence of years of starchy prison food. I reminded myself that he was the same age as my son, nearing fifty. This man was grave and comfortable in his own skin. There was no hint of the glib, overconfident offender I had met more than twenty years earlier.

I finally got to ask the question posed by his 2016 letter: "How did you come to live at this prison which is designated for youthful offenders?"

He described his recruitment for a program in which seasoned prisoners would be placed at MTU as role models. Once he arrived at the facility, he had been offered another opportunity: placement in the Calvin Prison Initiative. This was a five-year course of study provided by Calvin University during which prisoners serving life or very long sentences would work toward a degree specific to incarcerated individuals called "Faith and Community Leadership" with a minor in social work. Books, faculty, and tuition, as well as a computer, were provided at no charge by Calvin. The prison agreed to house participants together so they could provide mutual support.

Initially, he turned down the program, unable to envision himself as a late-in-life college student. However, by the time we met, he had embarked on that course of study. He told me, "Whether I am resentenced or not, I can lead a life of service. I now have a clear purpose in life, and it does not really matter to me if I offer that life in prison or on the streets."

I was moved by his declaration. It seemed genuine. On the trip home from Ionia, I said, "I am prepared to testify for Mr. Hammond if it becomes necessary."

Ms. Root later contacted me and said, "We have been able to reach an agreement with the prosecutor's office for resentencing Mr. Hammond to forty to sixty years. Your testimony will not be needed."

I asked when and where the hearing was. I was interested in attending, because, as a result of my involvement with Mr. Hammond's case, I had been asked to prepare reports for the courts in other juvenile lifer cases. Testimony about those reports was a possibility and I was curious to see how the hearings were conducted.

In January 2020, I attended Mr. Hammond's resentencing hearing. My understanding of the process in Michigan was that an agreement for a sentence of a term of years between the state appellate defender office and the prosecutor binds the judge to that new sentence; however, Shiawassee County's jurist had to be elected periodically, so the judge chose to have a full hearing before pronouncing the sentence. The victim's family and a friend spoke of how their lives had changed. One said that the victim "will never marry, have children, or enjoy his life. Ron Hammond should not have those opportunities either."

Then Mr. Hammond made his statement: "I understand nothing I do will bring [the victim] back to his family. All I can do is live a life of service that will honor his memory."

After that, the assistant prosecutor stated that his reasoning for agreeing to the new sentence was in line with the Supreme Court's decision. Actions as a youth must be balanced by conduct in prison. Only if the offender is considered irredeemable should the sentence of life with no possibility of parole stand. In spite of heavy pressure from the judge to retreat from the agreed-upon term of years, the young assistant prosecutor from Kent County stood his ground. (As an aside, I'll note that the use of another county prosecutor's office was necessitated by the involvement of the then-current Shiawassee County prosecutor in Mr. Hammond's original case.)

With clear reluctance, the judge then sentenced Mr. Hammond to forty to sixty years. Due to the tensions in the courtroom, the assistant prosecutor was escorted to his vehicle by sheriff's deputies as Mr. Hammond was taken away by Corrections's transportation staff. Outside the courthouse, I met in the weak January sun with the attorney who had represented Mr. Hammond; Katherine Root, the attorney who had brought me into the case by asking me to testify in favor of a new sentence; and Mr. Hammond's family. I was surprised that the family members present were unenthusiastic about the prospect of Mr. Hammond's parole. I was expecting them to be in a celebratory mood; instead, they were wary and unsure. Ron's mother, who had been the rock of the family, had passed while he was incarcerated. No one appeared to want to welcome Mr. Hammond home. On reflection, I had to recognize that the courtroom of hostile people represented the community to which Mr. Hammond would return and in which his family had been living. The young man they had sent to prison was a violent person who thought only about his own needs. If paroled, his transition was not going to be easy.

However, Mr. Hammond did not parole to Shiawassee County. Part of the Calvin Prison Initiative is a commitment to continued support on parole, including housing, books, tuition, and help finding employment upon graduation. So, when the parole board considered his case and decided to release him in January 2021, he went to Kent County and continued his studies at Calvin University. While most parolees change their major to social work, Mr. Hammond has decided to pursue human resources management.

I wrote to Mr. Hammond after his testimony at his resentencing:
As you know, I attended your resentencing hearing...While you demonstrated that you have thoughtfully considered the harm you have caused and recognize you cannot undo it...A life may not be defined only by bad actions. Especially those committed as a youth. You, fortunately, now will have the opportunity to contribute to others and balance out the harm you have caused through positive impacts on others.

Our letters crossed in the mail; he had written to me:
Thank you for attending my resentencing on January 24, 2020. Your presence was very helpful...Initially on leaving the STP Program I thought I had it figured out. I believed if I did the work and thought through situations that concrete answers would always be my reward. When I realized that is not always the case, I struggled. However, the belief that I could influence positive change in my life and future never truly left me and I continued to work. To my amazement hard work still does not always reward me with concrete answers. However, an honest effort and hard work more frequently than not end in positive results—although I do not know in advance what that success will look like. It took time for me to trust myself and the process. During this period, I was always grateful for your lessons which have been [sic] truly guided me throughout the years. Though I continue to wrestle with the fairness of my new opportunity, I will continue to have faith in the process.

He went on:
I truly owe you my life. Not only did you teach me how to take responsibility for my past, present and future, you also inspired me to find my true calling—service. The Calvin Prison Initiative is providing those of us in the program with a tremendous opportunity to serve, both in and out of prison. It is very exciting, but I would not be here now if it wasn't for you.

I can never thank you enough for preparing me for this moment. Prison by design is an uncomfortable environment to live in, however, thanks to you, I have known true freedom and peace for a very long time. I have been free from anger, free from resentment, and free from self-hate, and more importantly I have found true joy in helping others. To say you have been an inspiration would be an understatement...you have been a true role model in every sense of the word. Thank you.

His letters over the years document his progress and maturation. It is my hope that Ron Hammond goes on to complete his parole in 2023, graduate from Calvin, and become a contributing citizen of Michigan.

Bill Kime, Pam, and Corrections Director Perry Johnson at a conference (late 1970s)

Pam in the "Pine Box" at Camp Brighton with a coffee cup from her staff (late 1970s)

Barracks at Camp Brighton (undated, photo courtesy of Michigan Dept. of Corrections)

Entrance for staff and visitors at Jackson Central Complex (undated, photo courtesy of the Michigan Department of Corrections)

Michigan Dunes Correctional Facility (mid-1980s)

Entrance to the Michigan Dunes Correctional Facility (mid-1980s)

Pam looking for dust during a housing unit inspection at the Michigan Dunes (mid-1980s)

Pam in her office at the Michigan Dunes (mid-1980s)

Pam talking with prisoners outside the Rotunda entrance inside the Michigan Reformatory (late 1990s)

Ron Hammond in the STP yard at the Michigan Reformatory (late 1990s)

"The Network": Tekla Miller, Luella Burke, Denise Quarles, and Pam near the front desk of the Western Wayne Correctional Facility celebrating Luella's 50th birthday. She was the warden there (1991).

Michigan Reformatory. Left to right: the wall, G-Block (one of four wings off the rotunda), which was part of the 1877 construction. The Rotunda is partially obscured by an addition (called the front house) which housed administrative offices, the visiting room, the visitor waiting room, and the arsenal. The fenced yard in front of G-Block was once used for visiting. The sidewalk is for both staff and visitors, although there is a handicap ramp (not pictured), which is also used by both (undated, photo courtesy of the Michigan Department of Corrections).

Michigan Reformatory from the left, looking north from the Rotunda along one of the wings leading to an elevator tower with a gun tower overlooking the segregation exercise modules adjacent to I-Block (one of two "new" housing units built in the 1940s) with a second gun tower at the far right (late 1990s, photo courtesy of the Michigan Department of Corrections).

Michigan Reformatory Rotunda, east side, with the prisoner delivery door to the right side of the steps (undated, photo courtesy of the Michigan Department of Corrections).

Pam at the entry drive of the Michigan Reformatory with a sign created by the furniture factory workers which announced her selection as Warden of the Year by the North American Association of Wardens and Superintendents (2001)

Bill Kime, Luella Burke, Pam, John Cordell, Edna Withrow, and Sharon Johnson Rion at the Warden of the Year event in Philadelphia, Pennsylvania (2001)

5. WHEN THINGS GO WRONG

What had seemed like an opportunity turned out to be a difficult situation. While I was at Camp Brighton and as part of his "advancing women rapidly" project, MDOC Director Perry Johnson sent me to a workshop on prisoner discipline in Toledo, Ohio. Participants were from Michigan and adjacent states and the course material was interesting. The workshop highlighted the challenges agencies faced after changes mandated by a US Supreme Court decision regarding prisoner misconduct. Like many other corrections gatherings, evenings involved quantities of alcohol. One night, the bar featured Ladies' Night—drinks were two for one. I thought I could keep up with the guys but miscalculated. I made it to my room, stripped, and fell into bed without pajamas.

While sleeping nude is not unusual, TV coverage of recent hotel fires must have lurked in my unconscious. When my alarm went off, my alcohol-fogged brain said, "Get out! Fire!" In a panic, I wrapped a sheet around my body and exited into the hall. There I found fellow workshop attendees on their way to breakfast. Oops. I sobered up quickly, but my door had closed and locked and there was no pocket in the sheet for a key. I knocked on the door of the adjacent room and said, with as much dignity as I could muster, "I seem to have misplaced my key. May I use your phone to call the front desk?" When the bellman arrived, I repeated, "I seemed to have misplaced my key." Without comment, he unlocked my door. I didn't feel cheered when I was greeted by applause as I walked into class. It was probably only because riots occurred soon after this bad conduct that I was never held to account for it. My misdeed was lost in the chaos of the riot recovery period.

Not long after the Toledo fiasco, I was promoted to Jackson and then given a second promotion to housing deputy in the high-security part of that prison. I described in the first chapter how overwhelmed I was by that workload. In addition to feeling like I was failing at work, my personal life was deteriorating. My husband had also been promoted and had the stress of a new job. In addition, we had moved two children from his previous marriage into our home. The boy, older than my son John, was not biologically my husband's; however, the boy's mother was unable to care for him. His daughter, youngest of the three, was confused by the move and resentful. Our life was chaos with two working parents, one of whom was not present very much. My son survived by spending much of his free time with his buddy, Jim Christie, who lived nearby, and my parents, who lived within walking distance.

The older boy had emotional issues which resulted in destructive behavior such as smashing or spray painting all the Christmas gifts of the other two children. When his mother demanded that he be returned to her, we all breathed a sigh of relief. However, we resisted the daughter's return. The mother's history of instability did not bode well for a young girl's long-term development; however, fate intervened. While my husband had been supportive of my career initially, three promotions in five years had me making more money than he did and working crazy hours. The marriage was in trouble, and those two doomed children were victims of our inability to work through our problems. John and I moved to an apartment in Haslett, and I began to plot my escape from Jackson.

Although that escape turned out to be a promotion to be the first woman to head a facility for men in Michigan, not everything about the job was ideal. The relationship with Bill Kime that had started soon after the announcement that I'd head the Dunes was blossoming, but he lived almost two hours away. Sometimes we would meet and have dinner in Grand Rapids, halfway between our homes. The relationship was tested by one of those dinners. We had agreed to meet in the bar at a Brann's restaurant on Division Street. I arrived at the appointed hour, parked in the back, and went to the bar. So did Bill, although he parked on the street and came in the front entrance.

After watching Bill check his watch with increasing frequency, the bartender asked, "Are you waiting for someone?" "Yes," Bill said, "but she is often late." The bartender then asked, "Have you checked the other bar? She might be waiting there." And I was! What were the odds that we would elect to meet at one of the few restaurants with two bars? Instead of being angry with each other, we laughed at the situation and enjoyed recounting that event.

»»»»»»»»»»»»»

Another personal experience that started well didn't end that way. While at the Reformatory, I attended a Wharton leadership program in Philadelphia and was asked to co-facilitate a similar session the following summer in Denver. Always up for a challenge, I agreed to do so. The session went well, and I celebrated by staying at a nice bed and breakfast downtown. It had a good French restaurant where I had an excellent dinner. After dinner, I decided to go for a stroll in my red silk dress with a little black bag hanging from my shoulder. The block from the B&B to the main street was not well lighted, but I could see lots of pedestrian traffic at the end of the block. I lit an after-dinner cigar and headed out. After I passed a young man who appeared to be sleeping I realized I'd made a mistake—he was not asleep. He leaped up and tugged at the bag. The chain broke and the bag fell to the ground. When he bent to retrieve it, I beat him on the back with my lighted cigar, yelling, "You have no business stealing my bag." I recall seeing the sparks on his white shirt and hoping he would have to explain burn holes to his mom.

He ran off down an alley and I stood at the mouth and shouted, "Take the money but leave the ID. I need it for the plane tomorrow." My plea was accepted, and the bag tossed toward me. By then, the commotion had attracted onlookers, who expressed concern and offered assistance. I asked them to watch me get the bag in case the assailant returned. By the time I got back to the B&B, the foolishness of my actions had registered. "What if the guy had pulled a knife or a gun?" I thought. I certainly was not prepared to deal with that. I had left most of my cash and all of my credit cards in the room, so the robber got $40. I must have looked a little wobbly when I returned because the proprietors inquired, "Are you OK?" When I told them, "Not really. I just got mugged," they were very kind, gave me a glass of brandy, and offered to call the police. I declined. No real harm had been done and I just wanted to curl up in my room.

»»»»»»»»»»»»

Prison life can be brutal, and I got a taste of that in 1997. We had been working hard to keep metal weapons out of the hands of prisoners. That effort saved an officer's life. When prisoners fashioned a shank (prison-made weapon) for assaulting a targeted officer, the only material they could find was the kind of aluminum edging you might find around a kitchen table. The assailant stabbed the officer in the chest, but his sternum bent the blade and he survived. Two other staff were injured coming to his assistance. A prisoner inside a housing unit was seen giving a signal of success to others on the yard. We had a system to monitor inmate phone calls and, soon after the signal was given, heard a prisoner say, "We got him." That told us the assault was part of a coordinated plan.

We locked the prison down for several days and conducted searches for weapons and other contraband. Predictably, the prisoners threw contraband out of their cells so they wouldn't be caught with it, but we did get small amounts of marijuana, a few prison-made weapons, and other illicit goods out of the hands of offenders. Teachers and other non-custody staff delivered bag meals to prisoners in their cells. Slowly, we returned to normal operations, although it was a tense time.

I sought counseling because I had been warned repeatedly about the targeted officer's petty abuses of prisoners. He did not physically harm anyone, but he would not give showers when scheduled or would hold a man in his cell until all others had left for chow. There are many ways an officer can abuse his power, and even though I had asked the officer's supervisors to counsel him, and had even talked with him myself, he continued to treat prisoners badly. While I cannot justify the actions of the prisoners, I understand that they had tried to resolve the problems the officer was causing them by going through the chain of command and that did not work. Therefore, in their minds, the action they took was needed. The reason I turned to counseling was to come to terms with the staff injuries I had been unable to prevent, and, ultimately, to confront the fact that I could not ensure the safety of those in my care.

One good thing did come out of this incident. Because of information gathered after the assault, I was able to make a case for shutting down a religious group called the Melanic Islamic Palace of the Rising Sun. We felt this was more of a gang than a religion and had been keeping a close eye on them. It was rumored they were selling drugs and running gambling schemes. Unlike most religious groups, this one had no counterpart in the free world. It was a prisoner-made-up religion based loosely on the tenets of the Koran. Even the other Islamic groups, the Moorish Science Temple of America, and Nation of Islam, seemed to be wary of Melanics, who had a reputation for recklessness and violence.

I met with the group's leader and explained, "Your group will no longer meet pending review from the DOC director." That news was not well accepted.

In fact, the inspector came to see me. "We have reports that the Melanics have put a hit out on you and the deputy," he said. That gave me pause. The afternoon shift commander then pleaded, "Please stay out of the chow hall and avoid wandering around the prison during times of prisoner movement." I complied for a few days, but soon returned to my usual practices and never came to harm.

»»»»»»»»»»»»

On a fall weekend in 1998, an officer took a pair of trusted prisoners into the inside maintenance building to clean. In an escape attempt, they knocked him out, took his keys and radio, and left him locked in a tool crib. He came to and found the only window without bars in the building and escaped through it, injuring a leg in the process, but managed to alert other staff. The prisoners were still in the building, and one took the other hostage, but let him surrender after a brief period. Then the remaining prisoner attempted suicide by cutting his own throat. By that time, a squad had been deployed; I was on site and ordered gas to be administered to prevent the guy from seriously harming himself. While the DOC had trained hostage negotiators, this incident proceeded too quickly to use those resources. I do not think the escape was well-planned and doubt that it would have been successful;

however, the incident was another reminder that prisoners are always looking for a way out, and we could not become trusting or complacent.

»»»»»»»»»»»»

In July of 2000, I had just had my first sip of after-dinner brandy when the phone rang. The shift commander said, "About fifty prisoners are refusing to return to their cells. They are upset about the new yard schedule and want vending machines in the visiting room."

I called my boss, JoAnn Bach, and told her about the incident. I confessed, "I've had a sip of brandy but think I'm fine to go to the prison." I certainly was not impaired and felt comfortable dealing with the situation. She concurred and I headed back to work.

The shift commander and I discussed our response. He said, "We have armed officers on the roof, have removed staff from the yard, and have supervisors talking with the ringleaders. We have squads with helmets, shields, and batons being formed in case the prisoners try to leave the fenced yard. We'll keep these out of the prisoners' view." Some staff wanted to use the squads and force the prisoners into segregation. Since everyone was safe, I preferred to wait them out.

I reviewed files of the self-appointed leaders and identified a few I knew and thought would be reasonable. These men were brought to an office adjacent to the Rotunda. While Sgt. Pat Kelley monitored their behavior, I listened respectfully to their complaints. Then I said, "We are already planning to add vending machines in the visiting room. You need to be patient while we find and install them. The yard schedule is not going to change." They listened, shook hands with me, and returned to the yard. We gave them a while to share the information and then directed all the prisoners back to their unit. Participants were searched and admitted in groups of three without further incident. Some were later transferred to maximum security with misconducts for inciting a riot.

»»»»»»»»»»»»

The rare suicides of staff or prisoners were sad and always caused reflection about actions that might have prevented those tragedies, but of all the things that can go wrong in prison, the ones wardens fear most are riots and murders. As my career in corrections ended, I breathed a sigh of relief that neither had happened at any of the prisons for which I was responsible. I was proud that no one had been killed on my watch and that staff, as well as taxpayers, were spared the trauma and expense of recovering from a riot.

6. WHEN THINGS GO RIGHT

The misery of working at Jackson after the riots had a single bright spot.

To survive, I called on my gal pals. Luella Burke had become a friend when she came into the Camp Program as I left the first time and then followed me into the Program Bureau when I was promoted to Camp Brighton. Denise Quarles and Tekla Miller were friends from the Field Services part of Corrections. We got together while Luella was in the Program Bureau. Then Tekla became the supervisor of Camp Gilman, which had been converted to a camp for women prisoners. Denise was running a corrections center in Detroit at that point. We had bonded over our experiences as pioneer women in corrections and continued to get together monthly while I was at Jackson. Those meetings could have been bitch sessions, as we each had challenges, but we made a rule: "Complain the first five minutes and enjoy the rest of the evening."

I do not think I would have made it out of Jackson with my sanity without the help of those three. We would meet, talk, laugh, and strategize. Stories of who would help and who was dangerous were shared. Someone suggested, "Let's go to the American Correctional Association conference in Toronto. We can take the train." It was easy to say yes.

Denise and Tekla stayed at a downtown hotel near the conference headquarters. Luella and I, financially challenged, stayed in university housing some distance from the action, but we met up for all the conference functions and had a great time. I still recall us all shouting out the windows of a bus, "Untuck your dress!" as we were riding to a reception on one of Toronto's islands. A clueless woman's gown was in the back of her pantyhose. Even though she was walking with a group of people, no one had the courage to tell her about her wardrobe malfunction. These crazy shared experiences made us friends for life. Although we adopted the appellation, others first called us "The Network." We liked the name, continue to be great friends, and refer to our group that way to this day.

Just before I began my time at the Dunes, Tekla Miller, one of my Network buddies, planned a cross-country ski party at her southeast Michigan home. All the other participants were couples and she said I could bring someone if I wanted. Since I was just out of a really bad marriage, I did not want to bring anyone who was relationship material. I remembered, though, that my old boss, Bill Kime, enjoyed cross-country skiing and thought I had heard that his wife was no longer in the picture.

My call to him went something like this: "Hi, Deputy Kime. Pam Withrow here. Tekla Miller is having a cross-country ski party and I recall you are a skier. Any interest in coming to that with me?" I told him who else would be there. He knew Luella, who had worked for him, and knew of Tekla and Denise through their involvement in the Michigan Corrections Association, so he said, "OK."

As the fates would have it, the weather did not cooperate with the skiing part of the party. We experienced one of Michigan's famous January thaws; a glorious, sunny day in the 40s, which on Tekla's deck felt even warmer. I know that because I was very rude that day. Bill and I had a lot of catching up to do; we spent most of the party out on that deck, talking, laughing, and becoming a couple, even though neither of us had come to the gathering with that intention.

»»»»»»»»»»»

While I was settling into the warden's role at the Dunes, John was adjusting to a new high school. Fennville High proved to be a good fit for him. It was about the same size as his previous school in Haslett and offered him a chance to play football and baseball, as well as receive decent academic preparation for college. When I moved to the Dunes, I said to Deputy Director Brown, "Please leave me at the Dunes until John finishes high school." John had suffered through the long hours at Brighton and Jackson, the disruptions of a move, and two divorces. He deserved a period of stability when I could give him more time and attention. He earned his driver's license, got his first car, and was quite independent. We took turns making dinner; he handled his own laundry and helped around the house.

When I started work on this book, John reminded me that I told him, "I need you to take care of yourself and give me no problems because I am the first woman to run a men's prison in Michigan and cannot fail." His cooperation became an element essential to my success.

He told me that as a high school student he sometimes told classmates, "My mom is a warden." They would respond with examples of how strict their own mothers were, and John would then say, "No, my mom is actually a warden of a real prison." Today he leads the department's new-employee training section and commands the Honor Guard. He has told me, "I'm proud of your constant drive to change the way people think. The cognitive program you brought to

Michigan was the impetus for offender success programming that drives every aspect of our department today."

»»»»»»»»»»»

Several years later, when I moved to lead the Reformatory, there was not much going right. We were short-staffed, with officers transferring to newly opened prisons. Those who remained were still recovering from the '81 riot and the relationship between staff and prisoners was dismal. There was daily violence among prisoners and between staff and offenders, as well as an unacceptably high rate of escapes from the dormitory.

However, by 1992, I felt we had turned a corner. That year, dormitory prisoners assisted the city of Ionia and community volunteers in creating a series of wooden play structures at a park. The offenders set huge poles during the rainy first day and returned to the dorm muddy and worn out but satisfied with their contribution to the effort. They worked alongside Ionia citizens for the next two days. Later, at the dedication, they earned a big round of applause when they sang "Jailhouse Rock."

Dorm prisoners also helped me with high school presentations about prisons and prisoners; I had fun developing one that was interactive. I sewed together sheets to make a base the size of a cube in a temporary facility. This was the sleeping area for six prisoners, and, in addition to three bunk beds, contained three desks, three chairs, and six wall lockers. Prisoners could also have a personal footlocker, which was to be stored under the bunk. Strips of fabric were applied to the sheet to indicate the spaces occupied by the furnishings.

I would describe a typical prisoner day and then say, "Can I have six volunteers come and act out the process of getting up, dressed, and out the door for the breakfast meal?" The prisoners would then critique the students' acting. One thing the students did not consider was that theft was likely if all the prisoners were absent from the cube. It had no door. The lockers were cheaply made, and the backs could be pried off easily. Radios, TVs, tape players, typewriters, musical instruments, and personal clothing were sure to go missing if left unattended. One prisoner told me, "One man must remain in the cube at all times to guard against theft. We smuggle meals out of the chow hall for that guy." I suspect the officers turned a blind eye to this because they were unable to provide adequate security. If someone got ripped off, a confrontation could occur, and prevention made the most sense.

»»»»»»»»»»»

As the walled part of the prison became more controlled, we started to have visits from outside entities. In 1993, Calvin College developed a choir comprised of their students and Reformatory prisoners. That continued for a second year. Calvin also provided an educational opportunity called "Interim" with accelerated hands-on learning. Jackie Lyden with National Public Radio's Weekend Edition recorded a program titled Juvenile Lifers in which some prisoners and I were featured. She was way ahead of the times in recognizing that sentencing very young offenders to life with no possibility of parole was inhumane. In 2012, the Supreme Court finally ordered that all prisoners sentenced to life with no possibility of parole have their sentences reviewed if the crimes were committed before they were eighteen.

Then, in 1994, a gospel hip-hop trio, DC Talk, made a music video called "The Hard Way" at the facility. It featured prisoners in a housing unit and on the yard and included scenes outside the prison. It was a subzero February day when they filmed, but staff and prisoners toughed it out. A drum set and other instruments were brought inside and set up in a housing unit. Band members mingled with prisoners in many scenes in the video, which can be viewed today on the internet.

NBC Nightly News with Brian Williams and Entertainment Tonight also visited inside the prison that year. My recollection is that Brian Williams only came as far as the Rotunda, which is just inside the pedestrian gates, but which is visually interesting, with a soaring ceiling and several barred gates. His story was about programs for young offenders. For the life of me, I cannot recall why Entertainment Tonight was visiting, but clearly young offenders were a hot media topic in the early '90s.

As part of a Prison Fellowship fundraiser, columnist Cal Thomas came to the facility, along with 210 citizens who joined prisoners for a meal in the inmate dining room. People who had never had contact with prisoners or prisons had a chance to learn about their tax dollars at work that night. All of these were potentially risky events; however, staff and prisoners were up to the task. Michigan Corrections got some good publicity and I felt we were beginning a cultural shift.

The initiative of most immediate consequence, however, was the work leading to accreditation. While the American Correctional Association boasted that no accredited prison had ever been successfully sued over conditions of confinement, that did not excite staff because we were already in the middle of a federal consent decree that included conditions of confinement issues and more. To motivate them, I shamelessly goaded staff: "No one in Central Office believes we can achieve accreditation." It was true that policy compliance was not the Reformatory's strong suit; however, policies often were based on ACA standards and accreditation was a vehicle to move us in that direction.

In preparation for the auditors' visit, which would evaluate security and programming elements throughout the prison against hundreds of standards, all supervisors were tasked with visiting areas under their supervision and ensuring that these were compliant. In my case, that meant the whole place. Even though I was inside the facility more than most wardens and thought

I had been in all areas, I still discovered a space formerly used for a college program where supplies and equipment, including glass jars of specimens in toxic fluid, remained. Since the program was not operating, no one took responsibility for the former classrooms or their contents. I told the assistant deputy for treatment, "Get with the business manager and order a dumpster we can secure. You have a major disposal task on your hands." I met with department heads and confirmed that every part of the physical plant had a person responsible for it. We got rid of years' worth of accumulated junk. Even if our push for accreditation failed, we would have a safer prison.

Preparing for the auditors' visit, supervisors became skilled at checking caustic and toxic inventories and accounting for critical tools with shadow boards—storage areas where the tool's shape was painted a bright color so the tool's absence would be immediately apparent. We replaced some particularly dangerous cleaning supplies with ones less hazardous that required a little more elbow grease to produce results. This was not a problem; we had plenty of workers. The documentation required for the consent decree often transferred to ACA standards nicely. When the pre-audit was done, it appeared we were well prepared.

The three days of the actual audit were hard. Some thought malicious staff might deliberately cause us to lose a mandatory standard; however, I did not share that concern. My issue was that auditors bring their own sets of standards in addition to those of ACA and I worried that some unknown factor would cause us to fail. Fortunately, the few deficiencies the auditors detected were able to be remedied and a recheck found us in compliance. When the auditors left, I was able to gather staff and celebrate our success. We had confounded the naysayers and managed to get the oldest prison in the system accredited. And we would go on to achieve subsequent reaccreditations throughout my time at the facility.

»»»»»»»»»»»»»

Escapes are potential career killers, and all wardens try to ensure systems are in place to defeat inmate attempts to leave early. I was pleased when Reformatory staff foiled a plot one winter day. Prisoners had stolen kitchen whites (white uniforms for prisoner workers) so they would blend in with the snow after going over the wall. That was to be accomplished with thirty-seven feet of plastic netting that had been used to secure a crumbling dry kiln, furniture pads, boots, and gloves. The netting was to be used to get to the top of the wall. The pads, boots, and gloves were to defeat the razor wire above the wall. Fortunately, none of the equipment the co-conspirators had acquired was used, except as evidence of their plot. They did get out of the Reformatory—but it was to a maximum-security facility.

Weather was involved in another problem that turned out well. A heavy spring rainstorm caused a stream that ran through Reformatory property to become a torrent, which carried a large tree that smashed a sewer line that ran beneath a bridge. The damage was discovered quickly. I lived in the area and knew the city of Ionia was replacing sewer lines. I called a friend who worked for the public works department. "Can you help me with a sewer-line problem?" I asked. She dispatched a truck with two workers and the needed pipe replacement. I had, by the time the workers arrived, called my boss and alerted her to the problem. Before people from the DOC's Emergency Preparedness and the Department of Natural Resources's Environmental Quality sections could get to the facility, my staff and the city's crew had the line replaced. This was a time that local knowledge and connections really paid off.

Corrections work does not offer much good news. We are usually short on funding, work with disagreeable inmates, are challenged by employee unions, and called on to meet the expectations of communities, prisoners' families, the courts, and Central Office—and sometimes these expectations do not mesh. As a result, we celebrate any and all successes. Making and keeping friends, meeting the love of my life, sharing a professional relationship with my son as well as the bond of motherhood, and changing the culture of the Reformatory from "the Gladiator School" to a place where staff and prisoners were generally safe, respected, and encouraged to grow are the successes I celebrate.

7. PRISONERS WHO MADE AN IMPRESSION

Although I can confidently say thousands of prisoners were under my care at Brighton, Jackson, the Dunes, and the Reformatory, a handful stand out in my memory. Let me tell you about those men.

One offender was at Camp Brighton three different times during my three-and-a-half years there. Staff called this "doing life on the installment plan." I thought I had begun to know the offender well enough by his third visit to ask him why he kept returning to prison. He said, "It is the system's fault. I can handle supervision in the camp, but just do not like the reporting to a parole agent. When I don't show up for appointments, I have to move and quit my job because the agent can find me at one of those places. Then I get caught up trying to support myself." While this did not seem to me to justify his belief that it was the system's fault that he was returning to prison, he clearly believed that his justification was a valid reason. When this prisoner left the last time, the camp counselor and I called him into the pine box.

I told him, "We have a bet on how long you will last on the street this time." Perhaps the disclosure was what did it, or maybe he was just tired of doing time, but that prisoner is one of a few who stayed in touch with me when I left the camp. Every three or four years, I would hear from him. The last call was at the Reformatory. He said, "Hi, Warden. Just wanted to let you know I'm still out. I have a crew of kids selling candy on the street for me. I get a cut from the sales, and it is enough to keep me going." Maybe we had discovered a key to reducing recidivism; however, I think it was effective only in this one case.

During a parole board hearing at Brighton, a prisoner who had been part of a brutal crime in which a homeowner was killed and his wife badly injured told the parole board member, "I am responsible for the old man's death, but that woman was old and just died." The parole board gave him a year-long continuance on that and a subsequent visit. Prior to the third hearing, I sat him down and coached him. "You hit the woman over the head with a fireplace poker, resulting in her long-term hospitalization, which led to blood clots that caused the stroke that killed her. That means you do have some responsibility for her death."

At his third interview, he rather grudgingly said, "I am sorry the old woman died," and parole was granted. This same prisoner had served as the camp nurse, passing over-the-counter medications to prisoners with minor complaints and bandaging minor injuries. Due to the emphasis on work assignments, all offenders needed to be able to work; those who were too often absent were reassigned, usually to a northern camp. Consequently, most maintained good health. Staff noted, however, that there was a major uptick in the numbers of offenders reporting to the infirmary for medications. This change corresponded to the theft of instant coffee from the commissary.

The sergeant reported, "I have shaken down the kitchen and infirmary several times and cannot figure out how they're doing it." Because, of course, someone who worked in the kitchen was getting the stolen coffee to the infirmary.

Finally, a departing inmate clued us in. "The coffee is in one of the big brown bottles." And of course, the nurse was hiding the coffee in plain sight—masquerading as bulk medication. Since it rattled around like the medication it was supposed to be, and the sergeant had not opened every container in the infirmary during the searches, it probably would not have been found without the cooperation of that prisoner. The theft of the coffee was through the metal back of the locked cabinet in which it was stored—an issue Michigan State Industries seemingly could not solve as it cropped up again at the Reformatory dorm with thefts from offenders' lockers.

Two other Brighton prisoners were especially memorable. The first was a slight young man coming from Jackson. He had a shaved head and a large rose tattooed above one ear. I called him into my office for an interview and queried him about his unusual presentation. "Oh," he said, "now that I'm in camp, I'll let my hair grow out and the tattoo won't show. I acted crazy at Jackson to stay safe. I won't have to do that here." I smile every time I think of his creative solution to ensure his survival at Jackson.

The second prisoner was an attractive, well-spoken young man from Oakland County who spent his spare time playing tennis. He had robbed a Clark gas station near his home, where he was known to the staff, and ridden away on his bicycle. Naturally, he was located, charged, and promptly convicted. His family visited regularly, and since this was his first offense, he was paroled at the first opportunity. Back on the streets, he returned to the same Clark station, robbed it, and rode away on his bicycle. He hanged himself in jail while awaiting trial. I thought I had known this prisoner, but he clearly had some demons he was able to keep under wraps. Prisoners who had also known him during his stay at Brighton were similarly mystified at his suicide, so I was not the only one fooled by his sunny demeanor.

Similarly mystifying was the time when the night shift headcount at Brighton came up long. Staff feared being short, because that meant turning on all the lights, counting everyone on their bunk, and, often, searching for an escapee. However, no one could recall being over count. It turned out that one of the offenders had smuggled his girlfriend into the dorm and stashed her in a vacant bunk when staff made an unannounced count. I never learned the smuggler's identity. That was the talk of the camp for quite some time!

Brighton had about sixty-five prisoners earning minimum wage while involved in work-pass jobs in the community. One of the assignments was at a Holiday Inn restaurant in Howell. That was always a concern, since alcohol was served and the freeway was nearby, creating a double threat—drinking and escape. Because of these concerns, staff made frequent stops at the site. One day, the prisoner was not on his kitchen assignment when staff showed up. It turned out that the restaurant was short staffed and had started letting the prisoner deliver room-service meals. Once that practice started, the prisoner informed his wife of his new duties and she rented a room, so he delivered meals and more! He was especially sad when his work-pass job ended.

When the director visited the camp, I told him about another work-pass participant who had recently been a victim of a crime. This man had literacy limitations, so he asked a fellow prisoner to help him complete his application for a savings account at a local bank. When his monthly statement came, the prisoner looked to his earlier helper to assist him in deciphering it. Apparently, the helper also noted the account number and, when released, wiped out the balance of the victim's account. The defrauded prisoner came to the office.

"I want to file a complaint with the state police," he said. I took him to court the day his case was to be heard. He had to take the day off work to appear. Imagine the complaining prisoner's dismay when the defendant's attorney asked for a continuance due to his client's work schedule! The defrauded inmate complained, "This is unfair. I took a day off work and will have to take another day without pay for the next hearing."

I did not comment on his situation other than asking, "Did you and your attorney ever play that game when you were charged with crimes?" He stopped complaining to me after that.

Another interesting prisoner was an older man in prison for property crimes. We permitted families to bring in picnic lunches on Sundays during the summer when visits were outdoors. We noticed that this man was visited by his girlfriend and her children, who he stated were also his, on Saturday, and then by his wife and an older set of children on Sunday. If all the children had lined up together, they would have numbered about a dozen, with not much over a year between each. I finally asked, "How do you keep your wife from coming on Saturday and discovering you have a girlfriend?"

He smiled and told me, "Oh, they know about each other and are friendly. My wife just got old, and I wanted someone younger; she wanted to stay married. So, we worked things out."

Probably the most poignant story I can recall is the offender who asked to meet privately with me in my office. He was very emotional and said, "I have a personal issue to discuss. My wife is pregnant." I knew he had been in prison long enough that the baby was not his, and he acknowledged that. "My issue," he said, "is really with my family. They are pressuring me to divorce my wife." He continued, with remarkable empathy, "It is not her fault I am in prison. I've been down a long time and she is a young woman. I understand how she could have gotten involved." He went on, "I love babies and think we could be good parents to this baby. I want her to have it, stay married, and be a family."

I did not have any words of wisdom for this man; he was in uncharted territory in my experience. I thought then, and still believe, that he was able to have that conversation with me because I was a woman. He knew most of the male staff would echo his family's advice—throw her out—and he thought, correctly, that I would just listen and let him work out the problem for himself. That experience was one that affirmed for me the value of having staff of both genders as resources for prisoners.

»»»»»»»»»»»

While Jackson housed many violent and impulsive prisoners, Five Block segregation was the setting for the only encounter where I was genuinely fearful—even though the inmate was behind bars and could not get to me. He had been convicted of a single murder committed in 1970, but was the suspect in multiple murders of young women in the Ann Arbor area in the late 1960s. Although convicted under the name John Norman Collins, he adopted a different name for serving his sentence. He held Canadian citizenship, and there was an agreement between the US and Canada that their citizens could serve their prison sentences in their home country if both jurisdictions agreed. Collins's family had started the legal process for the transfer, and all was going smoothly until the deputy director for prisons, Robert Brown Jr., was asked to sign routine paperwork to finalize the move.

Bob Brown had an amazing ability to recall troublemakers and notorious offenders housed in his prisons. He knew of Collins's name change. He immediately realized that the natural life sentence (life with no possibility of parole) Collins was serving in Michigan would not be in effect in Canada. He would be eligible for parole in twenty years under their laws. Brown knew Collins was dangerous and should never rejoin the free community. Also, the families of the murdered women would feel betrayed if this prisoner failed to serve his entire life behind bars. Brown nixed the deal, and I was sent to advise the prisoner that he was staying in Michigan. He was smiling and pleasant when I started the conversation.

"I am here to discuss your transfer to Canada." His mask of affability shifted when I went on, "Michigan will not agree to that transfer. You will serve your sentence here."

The look he gave me made it clear that, absent those bars, he would have wrung my neck. I had never seen such naked and feral hatred in my life. I think I took an involuntary step back, even though I was safely beyond his reach. Believing Collins was not likely to forget this encounter, I took advantage of the special-problem offender process and had a notice placed in his file prohibiting him from being housed in a prison where I worked; I then initiated his transfer out of Jackson.

Another prisoner I recall from Jackson brings happier memories. As I made rounds, I kept noticing an exceptionally large and not very handsome Black man who wore pink foam rollers in his hair. Those rollers were not sold in the prisoner store and not part of the barbershop's inventory, so I was curious enough to ask the prisoner's unit officer, "What's up with the guy with the pink rollers?"

The officer was an old hand who explained matter-of-factly, "Prisoner ___ is doing life on the installment plan and, while he has a wife and kids on the street, he adopts the role of passive homosexual in prison. It suits him to keep house for a stronger prisoner who will protect him and provide amenities in exchange for services. In addition to sex, he'll clean the other fellow's cell and do his laundry." Oh my, the things you learn in prison.

I also ran across a former Brighton resident inside Jackson. Since the man had done well in minimum security, I queried him, "What in the world are you doing inside Jackson?"

"Well," he said, "I committed one too many crimes in Branch County."

He now had a K prefix before his six-digit prison number. Prisoners start at the beginning of the alphabet and get letters sequentially each time they return to prison with a new sentence, so he did have quite a history. The local prosecutor had decided to charge him as a habitual offender, which resulted in a sentence long enough that he was ineligible for minimum security for several more years. This encounter made me realize that we needed more long-term low-security prisons because the cost of housing this innocuous character in high security was punishing the taxpayers as well as the offender.

Another memorable prisoner was involved in an incident in Six Block. I had issued a standing order: "I want to talk with the prisoner before we sent in a squad for a forced move." Staff had to notify me in any case because they could not administer chemical agents without the approval of someone at my level or higher. Most of the time, I was able to reason with the prisoner, so he moved without incident. This reduced the chance of prisoner or staff injury. It also cut down on cleaning costs for the body armor that staff wore. I thought all these reasons were worth my time and attention. To the Six Block prisoner I said, "Mr.___, the squad is here and ready to take you to Five Block. How about backing up to the bars so we can cuff you and take you there without a fuss?"

His reply? "F___ you! Bring on the squad."

Six Block was a unit with cells around the outside of the block, so five tiers of cells housing over two hundred inmates overlooked the area where this prisoner was showboating. He had wrapped a T-shirt around his neck, preparing to pull it up as an improvised gas mask. His torso was bulked up with magazines stuffed inside his shirt and pants, body-armor style. Of concern was the knowledge that the unit was built later in the prison construction process; as a result, the cell doors were sometimes able to be opened by the prisoners if they gave a sharp jerk on the door. The shift captain was commanding the squad. Like in the movies, when a prisoner is before a firing squad, the prisoner started to light a cigarette.

I was about to give the order to deploy the chemical agent, but paused to ask, "Captain, is the gas flammable?"

"No, Dep," he responded.

"OK, let's go," I directed. Gas was dispersed. To my horror, the offender's head became a fireball. The prisoners watching the action roared in outrage. Although the flames had gone as quickly as they ignited, I urged the captain, "Get that guy. We need to get out of here now."

The prisoner was so startled that he did not put up a fight. He was cuffed and carried out of the unit in record time and the block officers were left to clean up the debris thrown in solidarity with the showboater by the witnesses to the flames. Fortunately for the prisoner, the fire did little damage—sort of like lighter fluid on skin. He looked like he had a mild sunburn with some loss of lashes and eyebrows. Apparently, no one above me read the incident report closely, because there were no repercussions. The prisoner did not even sue. I, however, had a stern chat with the captain.

"I thought you said the gas wasn't flammable."

He stuttered in response, "I was right, Dep. The gas wasn't flammable, but the propellant was." Small distinctions.

The last memorable incident at Jackson was a murder in one of the honor blocks. Eleven and Twelve Blocks were reserved for prisoners who stayed free of misconduct and held jobs. As Jackson recovered from the riot, fencing had been erected to control prisoner movement and keep groups of prisoners apart. Despite the efforts to restrict contact, the prison subculture continued to flourish.

Four Block, with the most violent general-population prisoners, evolved into home for the enforcers. Three, Six, and Eight Blocks housed those who used the goods and services provided by the movers and shakers, who lived in the honor blocks. The incident was the last of three murders which occurred while I was at Jackson. The first was because a prisoner had stolen another's coat and would not pay for it when confronted; the second resulted from a problem on the street. The reason for the last one was not discovered as the perpetrator was never identified. I believe it had to do with a struggle for control of the gambling, loan-sharking, illicit stores, or prostitution operations run out of the supposed "honor" blocks.

»»»»»»»»»»»»

I was dismayed when told about events after a prisoner was discharged from the Dunes. Discharge happens when the parole board does not want responsibility for an offender in the community, and, as a result, he must serve the maximum term of his sentence. The prisoner involved was a charmer and managed to sell some of the religious volunteers a sad story about his lack of prospects upon release. Moved by Christian charity, the volunteers (without consulting staff) gave him a job as a night manager at a local grocery and provided him a furnished apartment, complete with embroidered tea towels. He rewarded their generosity by seducing the daughter of one of the volunteers and taking her to Las Vegas, intending to put her to work for him on the street. I was glad to hear that she managed a phone call to her parents, who rescued her. As a result, we augmented our volunteer orientation to include warnings about discharging prisoners and a requirement that volunteers' contact with former prisoners be reported to the prison.

»»»»»»»»»»»»

At the Reformatory, employees of Prison Industries and Health Care did not report to me, but I was responsible for security in their areas, so visited frequently and got to know the workers and their workplace. During my first year there, a prisoner assigned to the furniture factory was missed at the midday count. We reviewed possibilities for his escape. I asked the deputy, "Could he get over the wall?" It was daylight, so that seemed unlikely. "How about the vehicle sally port?"

Vehicles leaving the facility had been properly searched, so we did not think he had left that way. The remaining option was through the pedestrian gates. These were a series of three sliding barred barriers where two staff would scrutinize each person entering or leaving the prison on foot. I was confident the missing prisoner had not managed to exit that way. As a result, I called my boss, the regional prison administrator, and told her, "We have a prisoner missing inside the walls. We are searching areas near his work assignment in the furniture factory. I will let you know when we find him."

Well, we did not find him that day. The next day we asked the state police to use their search dog, but again came up empty. By the end of the second day, the media had discovered there was a missing prisoner and Director Brown was losing patience. He called. "Withrow, the public cannot understand how a prisoner can be lost inside a prison for two days. It is time for you to declare him an escapee."

At some risk, I defended the implication that staff had failed. "I am sure he is still inside. We have informants telling us food is being smuggled into the furniture factory and believe it is for the missing prisoner."

Brown wasn't happy, but he let my judgment prevail. It was my good fortune that around 5:00 a.m. on the third day, the sound of a shotgun blast brought me to attention in my room across Wall St. from the prison. "We found him," I said out loud.

The prisoner had popped up next to the post on the wall adjacent to the furniture factory. The post officer shouted at him, "Stop!"

When he jumped outside the wall instead, the officer fired a warning shot. Since the prisoner had broken both ankles during his landing, he was not going anywhere. Staff cuffed him and brought him to the Rotunda to await transport for medical attention. I spoke with him before he left. "Where were you for all that time?" I asked.

"During the day, I hid in the sawdust bin," he disclosed. "At night I roamed around the building looking for something I could use as a weapon, but everything was locked up. I thought I might get the officer's gun, but he saw me, so I jumped off the wall."

That he had been hiding in a sawdust bin most of the time explained why the state police dog had not scented him. As a sad aside, when I called his mother to inform her that he was safe—but on the way to the hospital—with both ankles probably broken, she said, "Oh my, I am an orthopedic nurse. Those breaks will plague him the rest of his life."

»»»»»»»»»»»»

The Ionia Free Fair used prisoner workers from the dorm during the spring and summer. These workers were supervised by Free Fair staff, with Reformatory supervisors stopping by occasionally to confirm that all was well. During a slow time, civilian workers decided to use the prisoners to wash their personal cars, giving them cash for that service and even letting them move the cars. The temptation was too much for one prisoner. With cash in hand, he took off in one of the cars, bought liquor at a local store, and returned to work. His absence was unnoticed! We found out about these events when he returned to the dormitory, drunk, and disclosed the events of his happy day.

The year before I arrived at the Reformatory, there had been thirty-three escapes from the dormitory. Although that number was reduced when a razor-wire-topped fence was built around it, one memorable dorm escape during my tenure ended in a Los Angeles suburb when two escapees were captured after a high-speed chase. The driver of a pickup they had stolen in Saranac had thoughtfully left his keys and wallet on the floor of the vehicle. Using his credit cards to buy gas, the escapees had made it all the way to the West Coast. I learned about the LA events when my husband's brother called. "Guess what? Your escapees made the news out here. Want me to send the newspaper clipping?"

"Yes, please," I responded. As I read the clip, I reflected what an irony it was that the police were unaware they were about to apprehend prison escapees from Michigan; they initiated a traffic stop because the tailgate of the truck had been left down. That the prisoners blurted out their offense and gave up immediately was a surprise!

On another occasion, an attempted escape ended when one of the participants was badly cut by the razor wire. Rather than leave his injured partner, the second would-be escapee brought him to the front door and asked for medical treatment. Not all prisoners are bad guys after all.

Inside the main facility, I was talking with staff and prisoners near the recreation yard one evening when I overheard one prisoner tell another, "She's the one who flamed that prisoner down in Jackson, you know." That had been years before, and I was initially disturbed to think that some prisoners saw me as a person who would knowingly light up an offender. On the other hand, some thought I was too easy on those in my care, so I guess this was a way to keep my reputation balanced.

Another memorable encounter started on another day while I was watching evening yard. A prisoner approached me and asked, "Can we talk?"

"That's why I'm here," I said.

He continued, "I have a question. At other prisons where I've locked, the warden was always accompanied by 'suits' when touring (by this he meant other high-ranking prison officials). You are mostly alone when moving around the prison. Why is that?"

I responded, "I've found that both staff and prisoners are more likely to talk freely with me when I am alone." I showed him the batch of three-by-five cards I carried and told him I made notes of questions or concerns and then was able to follow up later to be sure these were addressed. He indicated he understood and went on about his business.

A few weeks later, I was observing lines in the chow hall. As men passed me, many complained about the meal they had been served. When all prisoners had their food, I went to the line. "May I have a tray, please?" I asked.

I received the same food as the prisoners. Then I sat at one of the inmate tables and sampled the meal, finding it bland, but palatable. The same prisoner I had spoken with on the yard was working in the dining room. He came over to the table and asked, "Do you remember me?" I acknowledged I did. He went on, "What are you doing now?"

I explained, "I had a lot of complaints about tonight's meal, so thought I'd see for myself if there were problems."

He looked pained and said, "Warden, I understood what you told me about going around without suits, but Warden, you have other people who could check on the food. You don't have to eat this s—." I assured him it was the best way I knew how to confirm the meal was acceptable, but admit I left him shaking his head. (This was my husband Bill's favorite story about my work in prisons.)

As I neared retirement, an insight about prisoners surfaced. While formal prisoner classifications systems often focus on a prisoner's dangerousness, length of sentence, need for academic and vocational training, substance abuse treatment programs, and mental and physical health treatment, I came to classify prisoners in a different way. In my experience, offenders can usually be thought of as sad, mad, or bad.

By sad, I mean they may have cognitive deficits due to drug or alcohol use by their mother while pregnant, abuse as a child, head injuries, malnutrition, or ingestion of lead or other environmental toxins. Sad because they were led into criminal activity by peers or older youth who took advantage of their need to belong. Sad because substance abuse led to criminal acts. Sad because they have no coping skills other than anger and violence. And sad because their untreated mental illness was a factor in their criminality. This group represents most of those who are incarcerated.

Prisoners I call mad are aware they drew a short straw in life. They see no way out of their impoverished and deprived situation other than through criminal activity. Often, they are bright and capable, but have no vision for a better life and often believe they are fated to die young. This group is small, but often creates problems for prison administrators because they foment discontent. The good news is that offenders in this group have the most potential for a fulfilled life when released if they elect to focus on self-change while incarcerated. (Mr. Hammond, who is featured earlier in this book, is one I would include in this group.)

The bad group is small in numbers. I can recall a handful of prisoners (including Mr. Collins in this chapter) that I considered irredeemable, but life with no possibility of parole is a good approach that will keep people safe from these men who have no boundaries and no wish to conform to society's rules.

8. PRISON COWORKERS: OUTSTANDING AND NOT SO WONDERFUL

When I started that first job at camp headquarters in Grass Lake, the car I had was not very reliable; however, I noticed that the superintendent and another coworker were carpooling from the Lansing area where I lived. "Any chance I can join the carpool?" I asked. It turned out that the coworker loved to drive his tricked-out van, so I pitched in a few dollars for gas and was treated to a first-class corrections education from the superintendent during those rides. He had worked for the parole board and in the old penitentiaries and was happy to share his experiences.

Specific to the camp inmates, he said, "These men are going home soon. It is our job to sort out those who can safely be returned to the community from those who present a danger." The other insight he shared: "Most prisoners will go home someday. It is the job of corrections to return them at least no worse than they came to us, and better if we can manage it." A few months passed, and I discovered a regular cribbage game at lunchtime in the superintendent's office. When a regular player was absent, I'd get a call: "Can you play cribbage today?" The superintendent noticed I was good, and he liked to win; I became his regular partner.

There were not many women in the camp headquarters, but Sally, the record office supervisor, and I became friends. She loved to golf; when the annual Corrections golf outing was announced, she complained, "I'd love to go, but women aren't invited." I looked at the flyer and could not find anything that specified gender, so told her, "I will go and drive the cart if you sign up to golf." We both went, had fun, and broke that gender barrier.

When I moved to the Program Bureau, the opportunities to meet people multiplied. One of the most significant was Susan Hunter, then working on her PhD from Michigan State. She went on to be a warden at a women's prison in Iowa, but her impact on the field of corrections was most significant when she became a deputy director with the Department of Justice. She was an early advocate for networking and increasing diversity in the profession and told me, "You must join the American Correctional Association. You will meet people from all over the country and get great ideas about prison management."

At ACA, she chaired a task force on women in corrections. Directors of corrections facilities were asking her for suggestions for women they could hire and promote, and we started brainstorming ways to get qualified women matched up with these leaders who needed them. "How about a reception at ACA?" I proposed. People were always eager to come to events with free food.

"But where will we get the money?" she responded.

"We will ask task force members to find sponsors," I said optimistically. And we did. Perry Johnson encouraged other directors to attend the first event and we continued to find sponsors and hold these receptions for several years. Private prisons were burgeoning during this time and I know of at least one woman who was poached from the Ohio correctional system to become a warden for the Corrections Corporation of America.

»»»»»»»»»»»»

Luella Burke replaced me at the camp headquarters, and when I went on to Camp Brighton she followed me into the Program Bureau. I was delighted to get a call at Brighton from Luella. "How about lunch in Lansing next week?" she proposed. My schedule was flexible, and I said "Sure." To my delight, in addition to Luella, I also met Denise Quarles and Tekla Miller, both then working in Field Services, where they had been the first women in their respective counties with male caseloads. We chattered like magpies and found we were like-minded.

When I was close to a breaking point at Jackson, The Network came to my rescue with monthly dinners. I recall Tekla telling about an interaction with the camp warehouse supervisor. An order of sanitary supplies had been cut without explanation. She called and said, "You didn't send enough sanitary napkins for the camp this month." The supervisor responded, "You are over budget, so I decided to cut paper products." When she was done explaining that sanitary napkins were not paper products but required supplies to manage her prisoners' monthly menstrual needs, the supervisor stammered, "I will send a truck tomorrow." Tekla was a bit smug about that success.

In 1995, I was asked to be on the faculty for a National Institute of Corrections-sponsored training called "Strategies for Success for Women

Who are Wardens." This was held in Cincinnati, Ohio, and brought together women from around the Midwest. What was most memorable for me at this session was watching networks form and personal relationships develop. Not long before the session, Michigan's Corrections Director Bob Brown had introduced Pat Caruso as the new warden for the Chippewa and Hiawatha prisons in Sault Ste. Marie. Ohio's Melody Turner turned out to be a kindred spirit. Both women helped me provide a successful national conference called "Women Working in Corrections and Juvenile Justice" (WWICJJ). I observed them at an American Correctional Association meeting as they recruited vendors for WWICJJ. "Hey, your product looks like something we'd like to showcase in Grand Rapids next October. We'll have over five hundred women at a national conference there," they said. "Do you have a card so we can follow up with you next month?"

And they did follow up and brought information about a wide variety of products to the conference. They also joined me as members of the North American Association of Wardens and Superintendents, as well as becoming personal friends. I recall standing with them on a balcony when Melody produced a handful of cigars. "Want to share?" she said. And we lit up and continued to add women to our line of cigar smokers, to the delight and dismay of those passing by.

»»»»»»»»»»»

One day at Camp Brighton, Director Perry Johnson and Deputy Director Bill Kime (my former boss) made an unannounced visit. "We were on our way back from Detroit and had a little extra time, so decided to stop and see how things were going," Perry explained.

Well, having the director visit was a big deal! Fortunately for me, the camp was in great shape. Hugh Leemon was the regular officer on days at the time. He had drawn up and posted detailed descriptions for every job a prisoner did at the camp. For example, the directions for a porter washing walls began, "Get a bucket," and continued with water temperature, type of cleaning supplies to use for scrubbing, and even that walls should be washed from the bottom to prevent streaking. This level of detail clearly impressed the director. I gave a tour, describing my routine.

"I usually take count and do shakedowns when the lieutenant is out checking on Work Pass or DNR crews," I said. "Except for strip searches, I do it all." The prisoners who were in camp were busy with school and work but greeted us as we toured. I guess Perry was favorably impressed, because not long after that I was headed for Jackson.

»»»»»»»»»»»

Before I left Brighton, we got the news that we would be getting a recreation director. Ordinarily, I would have been delighted with this news. Lt. Rupp had been handling most things related to the gym, and, given his security background, that mostly meant he climbed a tree adjacent to the window of the room containing the pool table and came swinging down when he saw tokens on the table to bust everyone involved for gambling.

We were getting a recreation director because Camp Pontiac was being converted to house women; no male staff would remain there. (As an aside, my new friend Tekla would be the supervisor of the camp, renamed Camp Gilman.) Most camps did not have a recreation director. The only reason Camp Pontiac had one was that our new employee had failed as a camp supervisor, but, for some reason, the agency did not want to terminate him. Instead, they placed another man over him. That meant, in civil-service terms, that they had a 25-level running that camp. Regular camp supervisors were civil-service grade 12, and the incompetent's supervisor had to be a grade 13 to outrank him, thus the joke that Pontiac had a "25" running it. There was not much enthusiasm about this addition to our ranks, but he needed an office, so I told the lieutenant, "Fix up an office in the gym for the new guy."

I was working a late shift and arrived about 10:00 a.m. on the day the recreation director was to start. He was in his car in the parking lot and rolled his window down a crack, hissing at me, "I will put in my papers to retire this afternoon." Not waiting for a reply, he left, spraying gravel all over the lot. I went into the office and found the staff convulsed with laughter.

"Alright, what happened?" I recall asking. Wordlessly, the lieutenant beckoned me to follow him to the gym. He opened the door to the rec director's office. What had been a small equipment room had been painted electric blue and was nearly filled with a desk painted kelly green. The floor was covered with splotches of both colors. A bare light bulb with a pull chain illuminated this awful spectacle. My lieutenant had succeeded where the corrections bureaucracy had failed for years. The incompetent would no longer receive a regular paycheck from Corrections.

»»»»»»»»»»»»

The time at Jackson introduced me to memorable staff. After I became housing deputy, the prison was recovering from the riot, and prisoners were able to move about more freely. As a result, assaults increased. Four Block was the most troublesome. I had been discussing the assault problem with one of the officers. He was interested in helping, so I said, "Do what you can to get these assaults under control."

"Yes, Dep," he responded. And Four Block assaults stopped, although assaults on the yard went up. I later found out that the officer had enlisted the help of a prisoner nicknamed Nine Lives—for the nine life sentences for contract killings he had committed—who had advised his fellow prisoners that Four Block was not the place for assaults. Unfortunately, I had promoted the officer to sergeant before learning of his inappropriate use of a prisoner enforcer to get the violence stopped.

On a night while I was working, late in the summer, staff reported that we had a problem on the yard. A fight had broken out and an officer in a tower had shot into the yard. He hit a prisoner wearing kitchen whites, so blood from the leg wound was startlingly vivid. Since that prisoner had not been involved in the fight, there was muttering about staff wrongdoing. Prisoners were milling about in unusual patterns, and some seemed to be trying to stir up others. Staff who usually patrolled the yard were removed to relative safety outside the fenced recreation area. Staff in Three and Four Blocks, whose prisoners were on the yard, locked their unit doors. Prisoners who wanted to get out of the escalating tension had nowhere to go, which further agitated them. As is often the case in these situations, information was hard to come by and conflicting. I was the highest-ranking official on duty, so went to the yard to see and hear what was happening. All the walking and talking I had been doing paid off. Staff and prisoners were willing to tell me what was happening from their perspective. The issue of locked unit doors was quickly identified as the most important thing to remedy. Since I supervised Housing, my order to "open the doors and admit prisoners slowly" was followed. Many took this opportunity to go lock up.

To the prisoners who were concerned about the wounded inmate, I said, "I will find out why he was shot; however, it is now time for you to go lock up." There was a rumor that the arsenal included Thompson submachine guns and I did nothing to discourage the belief that Warden Foltz would put those to work if things got out of hand. I called the warden. "We had a shot fired on the yard and an injured prisoner, but the situation is under control, and you don't need to come in."

When we interviewed the officer who had shot the prisoner, he admitted, "I targeted the prisoner with the white uniform because I had a clear shot in the evening light." The officer was charged with excessive use of force. This was not a popular decision, since staff felt any use of force to curtail prisoner violence on the yard was appropriate. After that night, they understood that shooting an uninvolved prisoner was not okay.

This leads me to recall another situation where staff seemed to forget it was their job to protect prisoners. An inmate in segregation with the nickname Lucky was in a closed-front cell because of his continued poor behavior. I happened to walk into the unit and saw smoke coming from the bottom of the door. "What's going on?" I asked. Staff replied, without much interest, that Lucky had set paper in his cell on fire again.

I ordered them, "Get him out now!" While they did so, and took him to the infirmary to be checked out for smoke inhalation, they seemed to share the opinion that he would have learned more had he been left to choke on the smoke a little longer.

When I was promoted to the Dunes, staff in Housing decided that I had been a tolerably good assistant deputy warden, and they wanted to give me a sendoff. They planned a nice event at the local Holiday Inn, and I invited my son, parents, Director Johnson, and his wife, Uyvonne. The evening was going along nicely when the Five Block officers came up with their huge boxed present. Things got kind of quiet. "Uh oh," I thought, "This is going to be bad!"

Was it ever! The gift was in honor of my newly single status—a full-size, male, anatomically correct blow-up doll. Horrors! Fortunately, I did not remove it completely from the box; unfortunately, many there had previewed the gift and were clear about the anatomically correct part and made raucous comments. I think my family, Perry, and his wife tried to ignore them. I was quite embarrassed, which, no doubt, was the point of the gift. In corrections we do not let anything go to waste; so that doll made the circuit of The Network in celebration of birthdays, anniversaries, or any other event we could make up to move the awful thing on to someone else. I am not sure who had it last, but it stopped surfacing, so it must have been thrown out. I remember Denise saying once, "What do I say to the cleaning lady if she finds it?" We had a good laugh over that one!

»»»»»»»»»»»»»

As often happens when a warden leaves, some of the staff are tapped to work at the departing warden's new prison. That was how I found myself with an assistant deputy vacancy at the Dunes and hired Carol Howes. Like me, Carol had worked in the Program Bureau. Before that, she had worked for the legislature; her background was broader than most in the DOC, but she lacked prison experience. The Dunes was a good place to gain that experience; additionally, I knew Carol had the moxie to contain the deputy warden's sometimes counterproductive initiatives. As he had in my case, he urged staff to run her out, but she was an excellent employee and won over the security staff who worked for her as well as others at the prison. I recall her telling me, "I would sit in the control center with shift commanders and watch you after you'd been away for a while. You'd find all the changes the deputy had made and put things back the way you wanted them, and we'd all laugh." She was a good listener and modeled the professionalism I wanted all to embrace.

To my dismay, the deputy continued to be an obstacle to my vision for the prison. When Denise Quarles, now warden at Riverside in Ionia, asked me to help her interview for a new deputy, I had an epiphany. Riverside was as close to my deputy's home as the Dunes, and he would get a one-level promotion if he became the deputy for Denise. She was being encouraged to hire a person with no custody experience and I was willing to hire and train that guy, so I made an offer. "If you'll take my deputy, I will hire Ray Tamminga as his replacement." That turned out to be a good deal for both of us.

I knew it was going to be a challenge to run the Reformatory, the oldest prison in the system. Early in my tenure, wanting to get a view of the physical plant and, remembering my days on Jackson's roof, I asked the shift commander if I could get to the top of the Rotunda, the high point of the prison. He detailed Lieutenant Doug Clark to escort me. After a five-story climb, Clark unlocked a gate and gestured to a wooden walkway that circled the base of the Rotunda roof. I wanted the best vantage point, so started climbing up the side of the roof. Before I reached the top, Clark said, "Ma'am, you are the warden and can go anywhere you want, but I think you should know that you are walking on glass." Why someone had decided to apply roofing shingles to a glass roof I do not know; however, I do know that I scrambled down with as much dignity as I could muster. Some years later, Clark confided, "I could see my career ending if you crashed through that glass and ended up in a bloody heap in the middle of the Rotunda." Since he was a fine lieutenant, I was glad I heeded his warning.

As for the other Reformatory staff, not all were delighted that I was to be their leader. Many of them were quite open about their distaste for a woman boss. In fact, one inspector retired, saying, "I won't work for any G—d— woman." I heard about his comment, went to his retirement party, and wished him well. The party was in Hubbardston, a particularly insular and conservative area of Ionia County, and I can admit today that I feared that I would be run off the road or physically attacked by a staff member whose inhibitions had been lowered by alcohol. Fortunately, I just got hard looks and a frosty reception.

On one hand, I was sorry to see that inspector leave, because he was experienced and had a good reputation as a security specialist; on the other hand, he was said to encourage physical retaliation for prisoner misconduct, an action I was determined to end. I was dismayed that staff seemed to revel in their physical confrontations with prisoners. One told me, "If a prisoner assaults staff, we drag him down the stairs by his heels. Then bounce him off the walls going to the Rotunda. Then shove him in a cell in the Adjustment Center." Since I did not believe violence by staff would engender good behavior by prisoners, I made a point of discouraging use of force and disciplining staff who violated that policy.

An opportunity was presented the day a prisoner knocked an officer to the floor in the chow hall. Other staff responded promptly and subdued the prisoner, face-down, across a table. The assaulted officer jumped up and slammed a closed fist into the prisoner's face. Not only did other prisoners report the officer's conduct, but staff confirmed it. I fired the officer. In Michigan, corrections officers have a strong union in addition to civil-service protections, so he was eventually returned to work and the prison ordered to give him back pay for the time he was off. However, prisons are like small towns, and, in this case, someone said, "You know the officer owes back child support." Social Services somehow got wind of the officer's impending windfall and diverted it to support his children. I thought justice prevailed in that instance.

Another opportunity to alert staff to the Reformatory's new direction came when I had a deputy vacancy. After conducting interviews, I saw the best candidate was a Black woman. Uncertain whether those in Central Office would support the selection, I scheduled an appointment with Director Brown. "I want to hire Jessie Rivers," I said, "but I don't know how you feel about having a prison run by two women." He knew her, of course, and knew she was likely to be difficult to manage; however, he did not share my concern about the prison being headed by two females. He replied, "Prisons have been run by two men for years. I do not see how having the Reformatory headed by two women should be any different."

Clearly, he was farther along the path to embracing diversity than I was. I hired the best candidate, and she was difficult. She was also a great role model and tough manager. I recall one incident in the visiting room when a mother was hitting her child. Jessie responded and pulled the mother aside. She said, "If you hit that baby again, I will call Ionia's Protective Services and they will put him with a white family here."

I would have been sued if I had made such a statement, but Deputy Rivers knew her approach would be effective. When staff tried to create divisions I sometimes had to go to her office and say, "Let's make rounds together. It is time to dispel rumors that we are at odds." And we would walk through the prison laughing while we talked. When she was promoted, I was sorry to see her go.

»»»»»»»»»»»»

And then computers were introduced to the Reformatory. It is hard to imagine work without them today, but getting staff to accept this new technology was a struggle. The first challenge was to convince my secretary, Barb Parks, to give up her beloved typewriter. I had to remind her, "You set the standard for support staff." She reluctantly learned to use this new tool. I am not sure she ever learned to love the computer, but she made the conversion with little complaint.

A bigger challenge was the control center. This space housed three shifts and the regular sergeant for each shift was the person most affected. Recalling the lessons from the Dunes and school staff there, I left the details to the three shifts, stating only that we needed to begin to use computers and that there were funds for remodeling the control center, but that all three shifts needed to agree on the design and placement of computers. Sgt. Pat Kelley was probably the most resistant. I think he was finally persuaded by this argument: "When we replaced the 223 rifles with AR15s, nobody liked it, but that was the new standard and we got used to it. A computer is just another tool we use in this business." While he was initially reluctant, I think that Sgt. Kelley would have objected mightily if I had tried to take away his computer after the first year. And staff did collaborate and develop a functional control center.

»»»»»»»»»»»»

Another activity that year was preparing for the Reformatory's reaccreditation. As in the past, I roamed the facility, looking for areas which might present problems if seen by the auditors. Two incidents are memorable. A shakedown of the recreation supervisor's office desk and storage space yielded felt markers that were contraband as well as a stash of prisoner tokens (prison money). There was no reason for a staff person to have the latter. The markers were permitted if accounted for as a toxic/caustic material. The absence of such a record could have caused us to fail a mandatory standard. While experience suggested we would have had a chance to rectify this problem in an actual audit, I was particularly unhappy because the responsible employee was one who worked in cognitive programs. I felt betrayed by his disregard of the rules, even though my rational brain understood there was not anything personal about the violation. I left a note. "The following items can be claimed in the warden's office: contraband markers and tokens."

To his credit, the employee did report to apologize and dispose of the items appropriately. He said, "I confiscated the tokens when I caught guys gambling. I didn't write a misconduct and used tokens to pay guys for extra work. I won't do it again."

The second situation involved the Michigan State Industries sergeant. This position was coveted because the hours were 8:00-4:00 Monday through Friday. The job was to ensure security was in place at the industrial laundry and furniture factory. In addition, it monitored activities at the inside maintenance building. This must have not been a full-time job because, in most cases, the MSI sergeant would eventually be removed due to some sort of foolishness. My involvement was the discovery, when shaking down the office of the sergeant, of a stash of skin magazines (all addressed to prisoners) as well as various contraband items including tools with the identifying numbers obliterated. Again, I left a message identifying what I had taken, although not offering to return them this time. I carried a box containing these finds across the yard to the shift commander's office.

Since it appeared the tools with obliterated numbers might be headed out of the facility, I told the shift commander, "Investigate the source of the tools. Deliver the magazines to their rightful owners or destroy them." Just as with the markers, the proper accounting for the tools was part of a mandatory standard and failure could have foiled our quest for reaccreditation. I like to think my example of taking a hard look, even at people and places thought to be compliant, helped us achieve that final reaccreditation.

Marjorie VanOchten, the feminist voice of corrections during my time with the department, contacted me. "I'm retiring and do not want a drunken brawl. Will you emcee my retirement party?"

"Yes," I responded, "with pleasure." She had served as legal counsel for the agency and attended wardens' meetings, executive staff meetings, and managed litigation, including the consent decree. In an environment that was still getting used to women as peers, she was often the lightning rod for women's rights. I recall an incident when a warden had used cardboard screens to shield the in-cell toilets when women began to work in cellblocks.

She inquired, "Are you creating a temporary fix because you don't plan to continue to assign women to housing units? Do it right. This is a permanent change." Men in the business feared her sharp tongue and acerbic wit, although she would skewer without regard to gender if someone disregarded the rights of any person.

The theme for speeches at Marjorie's party was her support for principled change. Bill Kime said a few words: "There was never a question of where Marjorie would stand. If an unpopular court decision impacted the department, she would ensure compliance and brooked no foot-dragging."

With gratitude, I concluded the festivities: "Thanks for always standing up for women. You took the general abuse directed at us and gave as good as you got." My recollection is that her party was more celebratory and less drunken than most. In any event, she sent me a lovely thank-you note afterward.

»»»»»»»»»»»»

Although we do not often admit it, wardens have favorite staff. In my case it was a pair at the Reformatory who had grown significantly due to their involvement in cognitive programming that made that list. Deb Davis was a corrections officer who sometimes created problems. Her work was fine. Her choice of paramours was not. The coworkers she paired up with were often abusive, and, when she came to work with the inevitable black eye or bruised cheek, staff would take sides. The drama was just not conducive to productive work. When she volunteered for the cognitive program, I was not sure I wanted the potential disruption, but decided to include her anyway. She told me, "That decision changed my life." She used what she learned about changing thinking to change behavior and applied the processes to her own life. As she grew and changed, she became a role model for other staff. Her personal life smoothed out, and she reports, "I still use the techniques when facing challenges." When she retired from the state, she transitioned to work for Ionia County, delivering cognitive programs at the jail and to probationers.

The other person is Abe French, who was an officer when he became involved in cognitive work with prisoners. He enjoyed the work, went to college, and completed his degree. As a result, he qualified for a case manager's job, and I was happy to hire him in that role. He was later promoted to a position in Central Office and charged with deciding what programs in the state would receive budgeted funding for jails and community corrections. Like Deb, he says, "Finding cognitive work had a significant positive effect on my life." After he retired, he developed training in cognitive programming and delivers this across Michigan as well as providing consultant services to other jurisdictions.

»»»»»»»»»»»»

I was working late one evening at the Reformatory when the shift commander knocked at my door. I admitted him. "Yes," I said, "what's up?"

"Well, Warden, I've come to ask you to put down your blinds for a while when you are working after dark," the shift commander said.

"And why do I need to do that?" I asked.

"Well, Warden, Officer___ is working post and you are a sitting duck with the lights on and the blinds up. He has a straight shot if he decides to take it."

"And what makes you think that is likely?" I queried.

"Well, Warden, it is only a rumor, but he has been a little unstable lately and been shooting his mouth off and we just decided it was better to let you know and for you to keep your blinds closed until he gets over it." I decided prudence was the best policy and followed his advice.

»»»»»»»»»»»»

I had been planning to retire. Keeping this quiet was important because as soon as staff know you are leaving, your authority diminishes. I had hoped to leave without much fuss; however, I had been at the Reformatory for fifteen years and staff insisted that there be a party. I did not want a formal affair and especially did not want alcohol served—that encourages bad behavior. The compromise was a pig roast in June 2001 on prison grounds. The weather cooperated and I was delighted when friends came from near and far to celebrate. My husband, Bill, presented me with a cookbook and an apron, announcing, "I am done being the chief cook." Director Bill Martin brought the obligatory proclamation from the legislature along with Leadership and Meritorious Service Awards. Administrative Assistant Robbin Bell created a lovely scrapbook with photos from the event and gave me a pair of huge retirement cards signed by many staff.

My son, John, and his wife, Kris, brought me to tears with their gift—a small silver frame with the message: "Coming to you in 2002." I was to get my first local grandchild in January. And that was how I transitioned from prison warden to private citizen.

9. TWENTY-FIVE YEARS IN PRISON: LESSONS LEARNED

This chapter explores some of the lessons I learned while growing up in the Michigan Department of Corrections. These are arranged in the order in which they happened, rather than ranked by importance.

1: Sit on anything written in the heat of emotion.

At Camp Control, in my first corrections position, I had an unpleasant telephone conversation with an employee at another prison whom I felt had wronged me in the handling of an inmate's eyeglasses order. I fired off an angry letter without consulting my supervisor. The recipient sent it, along with a response, to the superintendent, who asked me, "In hindsight, was sending the letter was a good idea?"

On reading my original missive, I was embarrassed. It was juvenile in tone and petty in content. I told him, "I was wrong to send it." He agreed. I wrote to the person I had offended and apologized.

2: Know what job you want next, tell anyone who asks that you want that job, and prepare yourself for that position.

While working at the Program Bureau, I was often asked about career goals. Since I'd started in the Camp Program and thought that the role of camp supervisor was about the best job there was, I always said, "I want to be a camp supervisor." I used the Bureau's library to research the department's organization structure and familiarize myself with policies and procedures. The time I'd spent reading Program Bureau files had helped me understand the questions the director wanted answered, and Deputy Director Kime was willing to answer any questions I had. To my delight, I was named supervisor of Camp Brighton.

3: When you want to try something new, call it a pilot project.

At Brighton, I wanted to try a prisoner volunteer activity at a mental health facility. It was something no one had tried before. I sold it to my supervisor as a short-term pilot project. In the press of business, my boss did not follow up on the outcome and Brighton continued the activity even after I was promoted to Jackson.

4: You must find a balance between what you can do and what you are being asked to do. If you flame out trying to do it all, you do a disservice to the organization and yourself.

At Jackson, I was overwhelmed by competing responsibilities. Policy required that I inspect housing units daily, conduct security classification hearings, respond to grievances, meet with staff, and respond to prisoner correspondence. The size of the physical plant and number of prisoners dwarfed other agency facilities for which those policies made sense. As a result, I used policy directives as a framework for duties. It was sometimes necessary to meet the intent of these to the best of my ability with the resources available. I let my boss know about my concerns, so he would know how I planned to operate. I visited housing units when time permitted, responded to inmate grievances on time, and delegated security classification duties. Monthly staff meetings were important and held regularly. Most inmate correspondence was sent to the unit managers who were equipped to handle prisoner complaints. Thank goodness the housing deputy job at Jackson lasted only a little over a year; I was almost defeated by the crushing workload there.

5: Do not muse aloud. Subordinates eager to please will implement wishes as if they were orders.

At the Dunes, the previous warden had a large desk, which I liked; however, his large chair just did not fit my petite frame, so I sent it away, mentioning to my secretary, Kathi Kars: "I prefer the wooden chair I brought from Jackson, but it looks pretty beat up for this nice office." The next day, that chair was gone!

I asked Kathi, "Where's my chair?"

She replied, "I sent it to Building Trades for refinishing."

While I was glad to have the chair—when it was returned—and it looked like it belonged in the new setting, I didn't have a comfortable seat for a while. Better to have kept that thought to myself until I had an alternative chair!

6: When you have a problem staff person, sandwiching that person between you and another like-minded staffer helps neutralize their effects.

Also at the Dunes, the deputy was an impediment to the changes I was trying to make. While operations were compliant with policy, staff attitudes toward prisoners were not respectful. The deputy set this tone, and since his office was inside with the custody staff, his preference prevailed. When I got a chance to hire an assistant deputy, I hired a woman who shared my values so she would back up my agenda. Custody staff reported to her, and she shared space with them, so was able to model and reinforce respectful interactions with offenders. When I got a chance, I traded the deputy to another warden and hired someone who would help develop the kind of climate I thought would promote staff and offender growth.

7: An injustice can be remedied with strategic action.

Membership in professional associations was a key factor in my correctional education. At a North American Association of Wardens and Superintendents (NAAWS) meeting, I rekindled a friendship with Sharon Johnson Rion, whom I'd initially met at leadership training in Colorado. At a later NAAWS meeting, my relationship with Sharon was cemented. She had worked her way through the NAAWS offices and was slated to be elected president for the 1991-92 term. She was to be the first woman to head the organization; perhaps a more controversial issue was that it would also be the first time anyone from the private-prison sphere would helm NAAWS.

Motivated by one or both factors, an Old Guard group of wardens put together an alternate slate of candidates which changed only one position. Sharon was replaced by someone they deemed more suitable. When she discovered this, she came to me both angry and upset—to the point of withdrawing her name from consideration. I told her, "This is not right, but we need to figure out how to fight it."

As we discussed strategy, she had a thought. "I know many NAAWS members, primarily women and minorities, who do not ordinarily attend NAAWS meetings. We need to get the word out that I need them at the meeting—and why."

We contacted all those we could locate and urged that they attend the meeting and vote for Sharon. Imagine the dismay of the Old Guard group when they came into the meeting room and saw it was full of people they did not know belonged to NAAWS. Better yet, when they presented their alternate slate, the person they nominated for president shocked them.

He stood up and declared, "Sharon has worked hard for the organization and earned her shot at the presidency. I respectfully decline the nomination."

Someone then moved the original slate be adopted, and Sharon prevailed.

Out of curiosity, I later asked the man who declined his buddies' nomination, "Why didn't you want to be NAAWS president?"

He replied, "I have sons and one daughter. The boys aren't going anywhere in the business, but my daughter is warden material. I would hate it if someone did to her what they tried to do to Sharon."

And I understood that this principled man who had run a military prison was also a feminist. Sharon and I worked together to benefit women in the business until we retired. We remain good friends.

8: Model the behavior you want to see, and state the nonnegotiables at every opportunity.

My nonnegotiables: Violence against prisoners is unacceptable. A clean, orderly prison is a way of demonstrating control. Giving respect is a way of getting respect. Listen.

When I arrived at the Reformatory, the culture of the organization celebrated violence. Staff liked that the facility was called "the Gladiator School." The prison was not as clean as it should have been. Staff openly referred to prisoners as "convicts," treated them poorly, and refused to listen to their concerns. These norms were the opposite of what I knew were important standards by which to run a humane prison. As I moved around the facility, I modeled listening to offenders' concerns, pointed out areas that needed to be cleaned, and treated both staff and prisoners respectfully. When staff used unnecessary force, I disciplined them. I challenged shift commanders with creative scenarios during monthly siren drills.

One I remember vividly was an escape. To simulate an actual escape, it was planned to take a school prisoner to the inspector's office so he would be missing during count. I called an athletic case manager into my office. "Are you up for a challenge?" I asked.

Without even asking what it was he said, "Sure."

Then I outlined the scenario I had planned. "Your job is to throw this grappling hook over the wall near the post overseeing the school modules. The officer will have been told you are coming, and he is not to respond to radio transmissions once you have arrived."

The officer was also instructed to stay out of sight in the post. The whole scenario was that a prisoner who attended school below the named post had made the grappling hook using chair legs and a braided sheet. He had smuggled this into the school by wrapping it around his waist. He would try to escape. When the officer was not visible, the prisoner would throw the hook over the wall railing and scramble up in the hope of startling the officer and disarming him. He would have arranged for an accomplice to be parked in the employee parking lot, which was not secure. After binding the officer's hands and feet with the braided sheet, the prisoner would drop to the ground from the wall and leave with the accomplice. Shift command had a routine of contacting posts to ensure staff were alert and present. During a siren drill, an emergency count of prisoners was taken. In this scenario, the failure of the officer to respond should have triggered supervisory staff to send someone to check on the post officer's welfare.

Some of the "tests" for shift commanders did not materialize due to the quickness of the case manager "escapee." He made it over the wall, simulated binding the officer, and dropped to the ground outside the wall before anyone even missed the prisoner or contacted post officers. This scenario was designed to remind post officers of their critical role, to test the unit staff's count process, and to encourage shift command staff to be alert to possible breaches of perimeter security. Staff certainly talked about the scenario, and the prisoner was missed during count, so I considered this a successful drill.

9: Attempt accreditation, even though it seems like a long shot.

The Reformatory was still recovering from a 1981 riot when I arrived in 1986. Staff seemed to think that "keeping the lid on" (avoiding another riot) was the extent of their responsibilities. On the other hand, I was a young warden (thirty-seven when I arrived) and eager to take this old facility on a new path. One advantage of taking on the oldest facility in the Department of Corrections after a time of trauma was that Central Office had low expectations. While most Michigan prisons were going through the accreditation process with the American Corrections Association, my boss said, "We think you should try to get Food Service and Programs accredited. Full accreditation is probably not possible at your prison."

With little hesitation, I fired back, "There is no reason the Reformatory cannot be accredited. Physical plant issues do not preclude meeting mandatory standards." I knew that the culture would be resistant to meeting the standards, but the challenge of bringing that old place into compliance with modern correctional practices was one I embraced. Accreditation is a process of evaluating all security and programming elements at a prison to see if these meet prescribed standards for the profession. Practitioners from state and federal prisons are the auditors and bring a fresh and unbiased view as they evaluate whether the facility is meeting correctional best practices. And we did achieve accreditation.

10: When your operation is headed in the right direction, reward yourself by starting a passion project.

Accreditation had been achieved and progress toward meeting the elements of a federal consent decree were well under way, so I looked for other ways to challenge staff and improve the prospects of prisoner habilitation. My early interest in prisoners' thinking was the impetus for the query to my boss: "Can I take a team to Colorado to get training in cognitive work with offenders? It is a new, evidence-based program for changing thinking and thus behavior."

She was open to that idea, and I applied for a spot in the next course with volunteers from the Reformatory. We returned and implemented a program (Strategies for Thinking Productively, or STP) that was validated by university research. When we conducted training, we would invite staff from other facilities to seed the whole department with cognitive concepts. Ultimately this program was implemented throughout the agency. It helped staff and prisoners understand that how you think controls how you behave. Examination of thinking that creates problems permits both groups to make changes to improve their lives. The utility of this evidence-based program prompted the agency to seek other programs that would support offender success.

11: Remember that you have a life outside of work. Maintain your relationship with your significant other, family members, and friends because you'll be spending your retirement with them.

Prison management can be all-consuming, and wardens often think they must be in control of every aspect of the operation. That need for control can lead to long hours at work and inattention to family and other relationships. And the need for control at work can carry over to personal relationships. Seek to separate work and personal lives.

12: See the possibility in each prisoner.

Probably the most important lesson is to interact with offenders with an eye to the whole person they can be. Offenders are often disagreeable and sometimes violent, and it is hard to remember that each one is someone's child who is likely to return to a community someday. The job of corrections is to return them at least no worse than they came to us; if possible, we should send them home able to be a responsible citizen with improved social skills, especially in the area of empathy.

So that is it for twenty-five years in prison. Sometimes I'll talk with other retirees and we'll reflect, "There but for good fortune goes any of us. We had a good family, good nutrition, and a good education. Our communities supported us, and we were expected to succeed."

While my idealism had to be tempered by the realities of prison work, I learned to use the values of the bureaucracy to support the changes I thought needed to be made to humanize the prisons I managed. The offenders I learned about in college classes became individuals with their own personalities and needs. And the staff who textbooks portrayed as tools to get the work done materialized as fellow humans with all the complexities each of us brings to any work. Together we all got through those twenty-five years and learned from each other. I have said I grew up in prison, and that is true.

ACKNOWLEDGMENTS

Thanks to Mission Point Press, where I found warm support and competent assistance in the adventure of self-publishing. Thanks also to my initial editor, Sharon Johnson Rion, whose gentle guidance improved the first draft, and to Tanya Muzumdar, the final editor, who helped me reshape that draft into this book. My husband, Bill Kime, insisted I write about the experience of being Michigan's first woman to head a male prison and encouraged me to retain the many documents which provided support for the narrative.

Thanks also to Corrections Director Perry Johnson, who determined that women belonged in Michigan corrections and took the risk of appointing me to be the first woman to head a camp for male felons and subsequently named me superintendent at the Michigan Dunes. His successor, Robert Brown Jr., appointed me warden of the Michigan Reformatory, the oldest prison in the Michigan system, making me the first woman to run one of Michigan's three penitentiaries. Both directors gave me freedom to implement programs and innovate without interference, a great gift in a bureaucracy.

Susan Hunter was a role model whose mantra on the merits of a diverse work force were prescient and true; they guided my staff selections. And, of course, gratitude is due to my other sister-friends, Luella Burke, Tekla Miller, and Denise Quarles, who propped me up during the Jackson years. Many early readers helped improve this book, especially friends from the No Name Book Club. You know who you are. Thank you.

My professional life was enriched by courses at the National Academy of Corrections, which is part of the National Institute of Corrections. In my opinion, both federal agencies are a great investment of taxpayer dollars. Organizations also improved my career experience—first, the Michigan Corrections Association, then the American Correctional Association, followed by the North American Association of Wardens and Superintendents, and then finally, the Association of Women Executives in Corrections. All offered an opportunity to learn from peers as well as professionals in other aspects of corrections work.

The staff with whom I worked in the Camp Program headquarters, the Program Bureau, Camp Brighton, the State Prison of Southern Michigan (Jackson), the Michigan Dunes, and the Michigan Reformatory helped me learn about prison operations; the prisoners tested that knowledge.

Those who read this book will intuit that none of the warden accomplishments could have occurred without the sense of self engendered by Edna Withrow, a purveyor of unconditional love. One sister, Tina, helped raise John. My parents, Charles and Edna Withrow, and other sisters, Chere and Kristy, provided support through the rocky periods of my life.

Finally, thanks to my son, John, with whom I grew up and who has apparently forgiven the acts and omissions of a young mother. He motivated me to get an education and a well-paying job.

ABOUT THE AUTHOR

Pam Withrow was born into an Indiana farm family near the midpoint of the 20th century, moved to Michigan in the turbulent '60s, and was a pioneering woman in the Michigan Department of Corrections. After a shotgun marriage, she returned to college, divorced, became a welfare mother, and completed a BA at Michigan State University. With the help of a bus-driver boyfriend, she began work with the Michigan Department of Corrections in 1976. After only two years, she was promoted to become the first woman to supervise a camp for male felons. This was followed by work as the housing deputy inside Jackson prison, which led to her appointment as the first woman to head a male prison, the Michigan Dunes Correctional Facility. She then served as the warden of the Michigan Reformatory, one of three penitentiaries in the state, for the final fifteen years of her career. She introduced cognitive work with prisoners while at the Reformatory, and it is now used throughout the department.

She was named Warden of the Year by the North American Association of Wardens and Superintendents, received honorary doctorates from Grand Valley and Ferris State Universities, and was inducted into the Michigan Women's Hall of Fame.

Made in the USA
Monee, IL
28 September 2023

43626092R00059